In The Long Run

by Bob Schul
With Laura Rentz Krause

Landfall Press
Dayton, Ohio
2000

Cover Photo: Bob Schul breaks the tape to win the 5000-meter Gold Medal at the Tokyo Olympics in 1964. *Sports Illustrated* photo by Neil Leifer.

In The Long Run
by Robert Schul
With Laura Rentz Kraus

Copyright © 2000 by Robert Schul

All rights reserved. Printed in the United States of America. No part of this book may be used or reproduced in any manner whatsoever without written permission of the publisher, except in the case of brief quotations embodied in critical articles and reviews. For information please address Landfall Press, Inc. 5171 Chapin St., Dayton, Ohio 45429.

ISBN 0-913428-82-5
Library of Congress Catalog Card No. 99-098094

Dedication To:

My daughter Robin, whom I love dearly, who has never seen me run in competition;

My first wife Sharon, the kindest person I ever met, who gave me all kinds of support when I most needed it;

Mihaly Igloi, the unparalled coach who showed me how to reach my potential, and who became a friend as well;

All members of the Los Angeles Track Club, a community with a dedicated life style;

and to Adidas, who did so much for me and for the sport.

My Best,

Bob Schul

The only American ever to win the Olympic 5000-meter gold, Bob Schul races into the record books in Tokyo in 1964. The contestants, left to right, are: Harold Norpoth, 2nd, West Germany: Kip Keino, 5th, Kenya; Michel Jazy, 4th, France; Bob Schul, 1st, USA; Bill Bailley, 6th, New Zealand and Bill Dellinger, 3rd, USA.

RECORDS HELD

American Indoor
3-mile, 1964, 13:31.4

American Outdoor
5000-meter, 1964, 13:38
Compton, CA
3-mile, 1964, 13:15
Compton, CA
2-mile, 1964, 8:26.4
World Record
Pierce College, CA
3-mile, 1965, 13:10.4
San Diego

TITLES

National Champion, 3-mile Indoor, 1963
National Champion, 5000-Meters, 1964
National Champion, 3-mile, 1965
Olympic Gold Medal, 5000-meters, 1964

Introduction

After the Olympic Games in 1964, I was convinced that the United States would be a consistent world power in the distance races. There were flashes of brilliance, of course, with runners such as Frank Shorter, Bill Rodgers, Steve Prefontaine, Joan Benoit, Bob Kennedy and a few others; but I did not realize until years later that I might have done something special.

Soon after, I came to the realization that I had indeed done just that. It was then, to encourage others, I started writing my life history.

This book has taken a long time coming together. Starting in 1966 I wrote the first draft. It didn't have much life, but my intent was to show others what I went through to become an Olympic champion.

Over the years I rewrote the manuscript four times. Finally I allowed a few of my club runners to read it and though they liked parts of it they found it too wordy and without emotion. When I bought a computer I started again, trying to add my thoughts and feelings, as well as my deeds, to the work. I tried to interest several publishers with no success. By then it was 1980 and I let the manuscript sit on a shelf for the next ten years.

Finally, I started again. Time passed, as did the 1992 Olympics. Then I realized that the perfect time for this book would be right before the Atlanta Olympics. I thought of the only five Americans who had won Olympic gold medals in the distance races: Horace Ashenfelter (1952 steeplechase), Billy Mills (1964 10,000 meters), Frank Shorter (1972 marathon), Joan Benoit (1984 marathon) and me (1964 5000 meters).

I was proud to be among them. All had been upset victors while I had been picked as the favorite by *Sports Illustrated* and *Track and Field News*; the first and only time an American had entered an Olympic distance race as the favorite.

I began asking people if they knew of a ghostwriter. Then one day, unexpectedly, I met Laura Krause.

In considering a ghostwriter, I wanted someone who would work with me and not rewrite the entire manuscript. I also wanted a person who was not too closely identified with running so the book would have a different perspective. I wanted my audience to be more than just aspiring Olympians; I felt I had an important message for many people.

After my discussion with Laura, I must admit to a few apprehensions. I wanted it clear that the book was principally my work, not an "as told to" sort of thing. She also had reservations.

I read some of the things Laura had written, and she read my manuscript. After some time passed, we decided to give it a go and a simple contract was drawn up to pay her for her time. We were both teaching full time and although she started to do some interviewing with me in the Fall of 1994, we decided to put off further meetings until school was out.

Before school was out in June, I gave her my latest draft and she told me it was much better than the previous one. I felt very good about that. We began work in earnest in July, meeting all through the month to discuss those parts where she felt the story could be clearer or where she thought more emotion was needed.

It was as if I was reliving my life at times. I must admit that some of the emotions were deep and tears would flow. I found it interesting that after so many years the emotion was still there.

Laura finished editing the manuscript that Fall. My thoughts and words were still there but she had streamlined the work while adding the emotion which had come from our talks. One area I insisted she not touch were the race stories for I wanted my thoughts and emotions.

The work had been cut down considerably and now I had to find a publisher. Someone recommended Dayton's Landfall Press. Alex Kaye had published a number of local authors, including some books on sports. After talking with him I knew I could not find a better person to help publish my book. We talked and Alex agreed to read the work and help me. Over the next year he suggested some revisions and I dutifully complied. Finally, we both thought it was ready.

But life brings about problems and the publication date was set back again and again.

Now, finally, everything is in place.

Preface

I was at the annual Dayton Teachers' Smart Retreat eating dinner in a very crowded dining room, when I noticed one of the participants looking for a vacant seat. Since there were only five teachers at a table for six, I motioned for the gentleman to come to our table. Gratefully, the man sat down and introduced himself as Bob Schul, a social studies teacher at Meadowdale High School. I also introduced myself, as did the rest of the group at the table.

Everyone went back to their conversations as Bob and I began chatting away like old friends. I mentioned to him that I was a writer as well as an English teacher and had published several articles. Bob seemed interested in this information and asked if I had ever done any ghostwriting. I told him I had not; and that although writing was fun and I thoroughly enjoyed it, it was far too much work not to endorse my own writings. Then I laughed as I told him he wouldn't believe the book I had in my room at that very moment.

"What is it?" he asked.

"*The Ghost In The Little House* by Laura Ingals Wilder!"

"That's quite a coincidence, isn't it?" Bob pondered a moment and then asked, "Well, would you ever consider it if you were to have your name on the cover?"

"Oh, I suppose so," I said, fairly interested in what he was saying. Then my curiosity got the best of me and I asked him why he was asking me all these questions.

"Well," he said, "I've been trying to find someone to write a book I've written. It needs a lot of work, and I've been looking for a ghostwriter for a long time."

"What's it about?"

"It's about me winning an Olympic medal in Tokyo in 1964."

"What medal?"

"The Gold Medal," he replied.

I was awestruck. Here I was eating dinner with a man who had won a Gold Medal! I was amazed. I grabbed his hand and shook it, feeling very proud and honored to be having this conversation with him! I told him so. (I never was one to keep my emotions in check!)

He just laughed, feeling a bit embarrassed, and said, "Well, it was quite a while ago."

That didn't matter to me. I'd always been a tomboy and was fairly athletic, running having been one of my favorite sports. I was very interested by this time, but we had to move on to our next workshop. We met later and discussed the possibility of my ghostwriting his book. I told him since I had never done this type of writing before, I would have to read his book first and then give it some thought.

Months later, after reading the manuscript, talking with Bob, and doing more thinking, I felt it would be quite a challenge as well as an honor for me to do it. It then took many more months to work out the details of our agreement, but we finally became partners.

Not only did we reach a business agreement, but after working together for over a year and getting to know his wife, Janie, I felt I had made new friends. Also, a most amazing thing was that Bob and I agreed on virtually every aspect of the book and often had the same ideas for changes before either one of us mentioned it.

I have been proud and honored to work with Bob and getting to know him and learn about his many disappointments and struggles those many years ago when he not only went on to win the Gold, but to still be the only American ever to win the Olympic 5000 meter event!

Laura Rentz Krause

Author's Note

When I started to write this book some thirty years ago, I wanted a history for my daughter, Robin, who never saw me run in national or international competition. Perhaps this could be something she could show her children, hopefully with pride at what their Grandfather had accomplished. Now, in November 1999, she has finished her doctorate in psychology and is married to Eric Thurber, a CPA. They live in a suburb of Seattle and at the moment I am still waiting to be a grandfather.

More recently I came to believe that under the present system no other American would ever win the 5000 meters in Olympic competition. Young men today lack the incentive for the lifestyle and struggle needed to win such an Olympic championship; other sports offer greater rewards of fame and money for the effort required.

Although the world has progressed in distance running, the problem is that we have not kept up. My winning time of 13:38 in the 5000-meter in Tokyo in 1964 would be equivalent to a 13:14 on today's tracks. Training has also progressed as we learn more about the human body. How many American athletes can run that fast? The answer is less than five. What must we do about this lack of great runners.

In this book I talk about Mihaly Igloi, my coach from September 1961 until August 1963. This great man came from Hungary to the United States in 1957. He had been Hungary's Olympic track coach at the Melbourne Olympics. When the Hungarian Revolution took place during the Games, he along with many of his countrymen chose to take asylum in our country.

It was a great day for American distance running and for me, personally. Igloi had been one of several men trying new training techniques. His were very successful as his Hungarian runners held all the world records from 1500 meters through 10,000 meters.

For thirty years I have used a variation of his system to train my athletes and have written a training book that is available. With this system I have taken good athletes who ran well in college and within a short time, six months to a year, had them running at a national level.

Bret Hyde came to me from the Air Force Academy after running in the mid 8:50's for the steeple. His times began to drop after a few months and in the 1984 Olympic trials he ran 8:25. Greg Reynolds came to me after the University of Illinois where he ran the mile in 4:08. After six months of training he ran 3:40.3 for 1500 meters.

Wally Saeger had run at Wisconsin and his two-mile race was in the high 8:50's. After several years he placed seventh in the 1984 Olympic trials in the marathon, running 2:13.

Eamon O'Reilly showed up on my doorstep with his wife and baby in the fall of 1967 asking that I train him for the 1968 Games. His personal best at Georgetown in the two-mile race was in the mid 8:50's. It didn't take long to see that he had talent and in the spring of 1968 he ran his first marathon, winning by more than fifteen minutes in a time of 2:16. At the time it was the fastest marathon ever run on American soil.

Gordon Sanders came to me after his graduation from Hillsdale College in Michigan. A year later Mike Michno followed, after seeing the success Gordon was having. Gordon progressed from a runner who hadn't broken 31 minutes to running 28:16 for 10K. Mike went from a 4:10 miler to running 3:43 for 1500 meters in about eight months. After the Air Force moved Mike away from Dayton, he continued to use the system and lowered this to 3:38.8 at 1500 meters.

There were many other open runners who attained national class status and through the years the Master's athletes on my club team have been some of the best in the nation. All were trained in the same manner but with added skill as I learned more through the years.

Within the next few years I'd like to move to a warm climate with good weather throughout the year to train some talented men and women for international competition. I have proposed a plan to the Track and Field National body to help build American distance runners to the point where many can compete on an international level instead of a few. For now I have taken over the Wright State Umniversity coaching job.

Through the years people have asked me if the Olympic race was the toughest race I ever ran. Far from it as the Olympic race was quite easy.

My toughest race was in 1965 after having been injured the previous November. After months of getting myself back into shape I raced in Toronto in May and tore a soleus muscle in my calf. This was two weeks before the National Championships in San Diego.

The only training I could do was repeat 100 meters. I spent the two weeks at the University of California, Berkeley where the trainers helped me immensely. With my leg taped I ran the three-mile race on a track that was pure asphalt; it was the forerunner of the modern all-weather track. It was all I could do to hang with the leaders but somehow I went to the "well" and pulled out a victory and a new American record of 13:10. After the first mile I was so tired I didn't know if I could finish but somehow I did one lap after another. In that race I truly understood what the human mind and body can do.

During my running career I tried to be an innovator, both with my training and with the sport itself. I was the first man to wear a heel on a pair of spikes. I had a shoemaker place the heel on the spikes I wore in the Olympic Games so I wouldn't stress my Achilles. In 1965 I organized the first Athletes Union, a group to have input into the National organization. When injury forced my retirement, the organization fell apart and it was many years before the athletes were again allowed into the power structure.

In those days a few people could control the big meets, such as the USSR vs USA, where attendance at the two-day meet topped 100,000 people. For many years the money disappeared and when I asked to look at the books there just happened to be a fire in which all the records were destroyed. I worked for two years to have responsible people voted into office after which the people in charge ran a very good organization.

I was also the first person to organize a clinic using Olympians. This happened in Las Vegas in 1966 and I asked five other Olympians to go with me to put on the clinic for the high schools in the area. Several hundred youngsters learned from the great athletes who were present.

I will try to implement my plan for training distance runners in the theory I have used for many years. We should have many people competing along with the Africans but it will take a concerted effort to accomplish this feat. In the 60s there were six to eight

American distance runners who could run with anyone in the world, now there are only two or three. The numbers should have grown, not diminish.

In starting the program, I plan to invite to a special camp twenty to thirty men and women to be screened for physical, mental and psychological attributes. I'd select athletes on their way up so the age group would be between twenty-two and twenty-eight. Part of their expenses would be covered by a corporate sponsor. I am convinced that with the right people, and the proper training, U. S. runners in all distance events could compete very well.

There is now an opportunity to bring track and field back to where it was in the 60s since we have a new director in Craig Masback. Meets must be staged properly to avoid boring spectators with too much "dead" time. We must speed up the big meets so events follow one another with precision and fans always have something exciting to watch.

My hope is that every reader will find this book interesting and insightful. Hopefully you will learn that athletes have many hurdles to overcome. Some give up but others will fight until their goal is accomplished.

I ran in an era where the official doctrine held that all athletes should compete for themselves and for their country. Above all they were amateurs and would remain so until their competitive days were over. But competition at the highest levels takes four to five hours training every day and I can tell you it is difficult to spend that much time and still hold a full-time job. You didn't have much of a life off the training fields.

We were working harder than most professionals (those who were paid) and yet we didn't receive the accolades they received. Amateurs never do in any sport. So I am not against changing the sport to make it truly professional. Some changes in how competition is carried out may also be needed. If that requires teams or some other concept to gain fan allegiance, then that's what we must do. The sport must change with corporate backing and more exposure. I hope to be a vital part of that change.

Bob Schul
Dayton, Ohio
December, 1999

ONE

The Beginning

I was truly a country boy, living on a 96-acre farm outside the small town of West Milton, Ohio, about 20 miles north of Dayton. I lived with my parents and three brothers, Norman, the eldest, Larry and Dave after me. We were a loving, yet a non-demonstrative family who had plenty to do running a farm but there was always time to play in between chores, especially baseball. An important part of my love of this sport was my Grandfather Keyser, who visited weekly from Dayton. On Sundays, Grandpa would sometimes show up with a new baseball, turning it over and over in his glove, ready to go.

Grandpa had rules, one of them being that Norm and I would never be on the same team, because we were the eldest. It was all right with me, though, because one of my goals was to beat my brother Norm in everything! Therefore, I'd begin my strategy as to how to beat him and impress Grandpa, whom I dearly loved. Well, as usual, there were lots of arguments, but Grandpa would have the last word. He never swore, argued with us, or raised his voice; just by his tone, we knew when to stop.

I loved competition and with everything my grandfather taught us, we played among ourselves just for fun (except for me trying to beat Norman). And in the early summer, I played on a local age-group team that competed against Dayton teams.

We were a mix of farm kids and city youth and were good for our 12- to 14-year-old age group. It was great fun to arrive at a game where the opposing city team would look at our sizes and laugh, thinking that beating us would be easy, only to see those smiles wiped off their faces as we went on to beat them more often than not. I really enjoyed those early summer months playing baseball, especially before the height of allergy season, when I suffered greatly.

I tried other sports, but didn't really excel in basketball and football. I made the basketball team, though, and was the sixth man my junior and senior years.

Football was something else altogether. I was 5 feet 11 inches tall and weighed 130 pounds. Being as thin as I was, I ended up on the "second team." That's the team for the kids who aren't good enough to play in anything except practice sessions! Our school had been league champs almost every year for the last decade, and our practice scrimmages were hard. I often came home battered and banged up.

I think back to those days of practices and realized that if nothing else from those months of grueling drudgery, I learned that I didn't quit when things got tough. It helped me "hang in there" for those later years when I was training for the Olympics.

Going back to my earlier days, track was the sport that was exciting for me. I went out for the team in the seventh grade and discovered that I could outlast my friends. I remember the revelation I had when I first discovered the love of this sport.

Being a farm boy, chores were always waiting for me even at eight years old. One of these duties was to get the cows in from the pasture before Dad came home from his regular job. So after school, I began a long trek across the road and down to the pasture. Half of it was covered by about ten acres of woods. During hot days, the cows would go deeper into the woods where it was cooler, and to make them even more difficult to find, they would lay down. To get the job done more quickly, I began running to find them. I ran up and down those hills. I loved it! I never knew I could feel so great. I ran through the field and down another hill, and then when it leveled out, sloping toward the river, I ran on that too.

Ultimately, as the cow path leveled out into the woods, I felt a freedom like I'd never known before. This was the first time that I'd run when it was not allergy season, and I felt I could do it forever. What a powerful awakening. It was after the first frost that I felt transformed, metamorphosed it seemed, into a human ball of energy. I was free, free from the confinement, the illness, the suffocating feeling, the swelling in my lungs. I could actually breathe without any hindrance. (For the rest of my running career I was to use this after-frost time to maximize my training and potential.)

As I was soaking up all these magnificent feelings, I wished Norman could see me now. I always felt so bad that I couldn't play or work like my brothers could during the allergy season. Norman would tell me when we were by ourselves that I was so sickly, I'd never be a good athlete. I felt inadequate and ashamed because Norm acted like I was shirking my duties.

"You can't work like me and Larry can," he'd say. "You're always sick." He even remembered when I almost died at about 15 months old; maybe he just remembered my mother telling me the story.

"He's turning blue!" My mother hurriedly reacted with quick wit as my blue body reflected the oxygen being cut off from my windpipe. Frightened, yet in control, groping fingers tried to bring life back into my body. She forced her finger down my throat to dislodge the mucous that was suffocating me. This happened through forced retching. As she scooped the deadly phlegm from my mouth and I inhaled, she saw life come back into my small body and my color return to normal. She sat there stunned after this near-death situation as I fell into a much needed-slumber. This made a deep impression on the four-year-old Norm, especially for me to have this near-death experience again in the next six months. He always saw me as a weakling after that.

Mom said she never really spent time worrying about whether or not I'd die from my allergies because I would get into other precarious situations that could jeopardize my life just as easily. She said she was amazed how I could be so sick and weak in one situation and then have energy for another little adventure such as the time she glanced out the window while she was washing dinner dishes one evening.

What she saw in the barn area was me at age four standing near the top of a four-story high ladder Dad had left leaning against the side of the barn. I was all set to step onto the roof Mom rushed out and called me as calmly as she could, considering the situation. I stopped and looked out at her far below.

"How is it up there, Bobby?"

"Fine Mommy, I like this. I can see a long way!"

"That's good, but you need to come down now."

She wasn't good with heights and wasn't about to climb very far, but she edged up the ladder, talking to me until we met on the rungs. After the careful descent, she just shook her head and held me close thinking this ongoing life-and-death drama was a far cry from her training as a teacher.

Before she began the difficult work of being a farm wife, Mom had graduated from Wittenburg University in Springfield, Ohio and taught near the Hamilton, Ohio area. Dad was farming close by for Governor Cox. He learned about a school teacher named Katherine Keyser and wanted to meet her.

One day he took his hunting dogs out to look for raccoons, near the school property. He hunted with the dogs, then let them run off to find the raccoons. Inside, he went to meet Miss Keyser. They were married two years later.

They moved to a West Milton farm which was bought by my mother's father. Dad didn't like this indebtedness to my grandfather and worked hard to pay off this debt within seven years. Dad never again accrued a debt. Everything he bought -- cars, farm equipment, household goods, even their new house prior to his retirement -- was paid for in cash. This was quite a feat during those post-depression years, but we all worked hard pulling together as a family to help save whenever we could.

During World War II, we had ration stamps, which were given to every member of the family. I felt some pride that I could give Mom my stamps for coffee and especially sugar so she could use as much as she wanted making jellies and jams and other things we raised or harvested.

Another way we helped during the war was when the government in 1943 had all the rural schools save milkweed pods for them. These pods were eventually used in the making of life preservers. The seeds inside the pod were carried by a fluffy material.

It was this fluff inside the pods that was used for the preservers. It had a buoyancy factor unparalleled by anything else at that time. We gave the unopened pods to the school, then someone from the military would pick them up. Persons who brought in the most pods would get a certificate. It was with such a great feeling of pride that I did this task of helping our soldiers, especially since I was just six at this time of the war.

My two younger brothers, Larry and Dave, were born in 1939 and 1942, and they were healthy boys. So all of us, in our own ways, did what we could and what was asked of us on the farm.

With helping Dad conserve money, doing all the necessary duties around the house and raising four sons, Mom had her hands completely full. It was quite a dilemma then, when she was approached by the West Milton school principal to return to teaching due to a lack of teachers.

The shortage was so severe that he told Mom that Dave would be allowed to begin the first grade at the age of four if only she would return to teaching. After talking with Dad, they agreed it would be a good thing to do. Mom then included her job as another duty in a difficult farm life. She remained in teaching until her retirement 30 years later.

As I said, I always looked up to Norm, even though we were in constant competition with each other. He was the brains of the family and could handle a situation on his own in regards to small crises befitting younger brothers.

Once when we were in grade school, a ruffian neighbor took my report card and held it flat against the school bus window, mocking me as I was trying to grab it. In his teasing, it slipped down the well of the window. I was horrified to see my report card disappear as the ruffian sat back in his seat, laughing. I was worried sick about retuning to school without my card and pictured the outraged teacher as I stood before her. I was far too shy to talk to her and I felt miserable.

Norman told me not to worry, that he'd go with me to my class and explain things to the teacher. He calmed my fears, went with me to my class and resolved my problem. Norm grew another inch that day in my eyes. In many ways I wanted to be like him and even more so to have him be proud of me. At that time, I never would have thought that my dream would some day come true.

In addition to wanting my brothers to admire me, I really wanted my father's respect as well. Dad didn't accept my being ill easily, although he never said so. I could sense his disbelief that I was such a sickly child and couldn't do what the rest of the "men" in the family could do. I felt this inadequacy in Dad's presence often although I did do all my chores; that is, until the allergy season from mid-July to the first frost in September. This was the most severe time of year for my health.

In working with my brothers, I tried different things to combat my breathing problem, such as when I drove the tractor while they loaded the hay. I wore my Uncle Keyser's old World War I gas mask to help suppress the allergies. I drove the tractor between two rows and Dad would go from one side to the other, tossing the loose hay onto the wagon. Norman and Larry would stomp down the hay in the wagon. My wheezing would start before too long and by the end of the day, I really suffered. Dave told me a few years ago that it was frightening for him to hear me trying to breathe from across the hall, that he was afraid I wouldn't live through the night.

When I would get back to the house, I felt like I could barely make it. Mom would have a medicine powder lit in my room to help me breathe. This powder emitted a vapor that the doctor said would help clear my lungs. It really didn't seem to help. I'd just lay there in my bed, wheezing, watching that little snake-like ash catch fire a little bit at a time, giving a little "poof" and smoke would curl toward the ceiling. An hour later it had burned itself out. I was in misery and felt like I was suffocating. My bronchial tubes were so swollen that I felt that every breath I took would be my last. But I knew it was best to stay relaxed and under the circumstances that took a lot of discipline. After a few hours my breathing would become better and I would fall asleep from sheer exhaustion.

After a bout with this, I'd awaken in the morning with my eyes matted shut and couldn't even begin to open them. Mom would leave a little boric acid by my bedside, so I'd reach over, groping around trying to find the solution and the cotton to dab at my eyes until the crusting loosened up. Sometimes, in trying to find the stuff, I'd knock it over. Then I'd get frustrated and try to open my eyes, which hurt plenty. The tears would come and soften the dried mucous. I'd finish wiping away the crust, and finally I would painfully be able to open my eyes. There was no time for coddling during these times and I never thought too much about it. It wasn't that I got used to it, I didn't. In fact, I hated those times which lasted for six weeks or more. When I got up I just went ahead and tried to make the day as normal as possible, hoping beyond hope that today would be better than yesterday. Sometimes it was and sometimes it was worse. It all depended on the weather and the pollen count.

A desire to do my best was always there because I felt that everyone was watching me. I wanted to show my family that I could do something other than being sick all the time. Therefore, having them be proud of me was constantly on my mind.

In junior and senior high school, I never felt I excelled in sports, even when I was succeeding. I felt that way through my high school career, just doing my best and hoping to win. I was always surprised when I won and found my body could do so much more than I thought it could in spite of my allergies. When I first starting running, I don't think my father thought my body could do much, and he seemed surprised when I did well. He didn't get excited about my wins, not in the "way to go, Tiger" sort of way, but I could see the pride in his eyes.

Dad and Mom both were easy going and hard working people. Dad was a strong, wiry man, very huge in my eyes. He worked harder than two men. His job away from the farm was at General Motors. He would go to that job after having milked 20 cows by hand from 3 to 5 a.m. He would finish this chore, quickly take a bath, eat breakfast, and off he'd drive to GM, picking up co-workers along the way. He'd leave about 5:30 a.m. even though his shift started about 7:20; his ethic for working hard and being loyal to his company had him at his job and ready to work 30 minutes before his shift started.

After a hard day's work he'd come home and milk those same 20 cows from 4:30 to 6:30 p.m. Although we'd never hear him complain, I'll bet he hated those cows at times.

Because running a good farm meant having a good schedule, Mom had to have dinner ready by 4 p.m. and with all her regular farm chores, plus teaching, she really worked just as hard as Dad. Just preparing the dinners was a great task. She would either prepare beef or fried chicken, great chicken that we raised and butchered.

I remember the first time, about the age of five, I ever saw Dad kill a chicken. We walked around the barnyard looking among the flock of clucking chickens for a nice, plump one. He'd then grab one in his strong hands with me trotting right along at his side, anxious to take part in this adventure. I was a typical boy in this respect, looking for the odd and bizarre and I sure found it.

Dad placed the chicken's head between the nails of a board which was on the ground. He held the feet, pulled the chicken taut, so its neck would be stretched out over the board about as far as he could without tearing its head off, and with one swift WHAPT! down came the hatchet. Off the head flew and as Dad let go, the chicken ran around the yard for about 20 seconds before it finally keeled over. I felt ill and so-o sorry for that chicken.

From the barnyard I followed Dad toward the house where Mom had the hot water prepared for the de-feathering. Because we had no hot water heater in those days, the water had to be boiled on our old coal stove. Dad would carry the large pot outside and plop that decapitated chicken into the hot water. In the pot it stayed, until the feathers were fairly well loosened. Out she came, and before I knew it, Dad plucked those feathers off that chicken like a musician plucking a harp. Although I felt a little uneasy about this whole business, I knew the end result would be mouth-watering fried chicken that night. Even at this young age, I knew to focus on a good end result.

It was years later that I had to team to do the butchering myself I didn't like it at all, but I remembered not to let my negative feelings get in the way of an important goal. As you can see, my father certainly played a great part in this philosophy. In the meantime, while awaiting opportunities to achieve more important things in life, I had to content myself in routine tasks.

Putting all the prepared food onto the table was quite an undertaking, and I was quite able to help with that. Along with the brown, fried chicken, we'd have whatever would be in season: yellow sweet corn, green snap beans, baby limas, red beets, whatever would be the pick of the day. Along with all of these healthy vegetables, Mom baked her own bread and churned her own sweet butter. Before we could even sit down to eat, our mouths were watering, anxious to begin our feast. No words were spoken for quite a while as we ate our fill of this delicious food.

All that hard work to prepare this dinner, and it only took 30 minutes to eat; that is, it took Dad 30 minutes to eat. He would eat, finish up, push back his chair, and go back out to the barn to milk the cows. He never said anything about us boys rushing out, so we would take an extra ten guilty minutes before we went about our chores.

Norman, Larry and Dave usually went on to their individual chores as I went ahead to do mine. Unfortunately, you never knew what mishaps were about to occur and one was very near at hand.

One of my chores was to cut corn for the cows so that they could chew it easily. I was using a machete-like corn knife, holding an ear, hacking it in half, when I slipped. Instead of cutting the corn, I hacked my finger. I could see the bone through the deep gash. It didn't bleed and it didn't hurt, although it was at the knuckle. All I thought of was that Dad sure was going to be mad at me for doing this. I then ran to the front part of the house and hid underneath the porch, staring at my finger. I wasn't there too long before my brothers were calling for me.

Larry finally saw me sitting under there in the dark and yelled to Dad in a tone that said, "You're going to get it now for not doing your chores." Dad stooped over and asked why I was under the porch. I showed him my gashed finger. He looked at it, took me inside, washed it up, and put tape over it. All he ever said about that incident was, "I'll cut the rest of the corn."

That's the way it was on the farm; cut fingers; hacked chickens and lots of work.

Everything was taken in stride. I felt really ashamed to have cut my finger and fought even more with Norm, vying for our younger brothers' attention; that is, being the big hero in their eyes.

There was one time in particular that I held my own in this "Who's the Best Big Brother?" competition.

Norm and I had a spat over something. I ran away and was teasing him from behind the bushes. He was so angry he threw stones at me. Whack! right in the head with a rock, and again I had a gash in my body. I ran into the house shouting that Norman hit me with a rock. Mom looked at my head and saw that it was bleeding profusely.

It shut me up when she said, "We'd better call the doctor."

"A doctor," I said "Can't you just put a band-aid on it?"

I watched my mother wide-eyed as she called on our cranking telephone to old Doc Pearson, who came right out to the farm, black bag and all. He sat me down on a three-footed stool close to the coal burning stove and told my father to put on a pot of water in which to sterilize his instruments. Although I loved adventure, this was not what I had in mind. I was terrified. He took those instruments out one by one. As they were boiling, he needed to cut the hair around my wound. Dad got out his straight razor, Doc put antiseptic on cotton swabs to wash out the gash. He then laid the instruments on a cloth.

He said, "This is going to hurt." I gulped, my brothers stared, my parents said nothing. He took the needle, stuck it into my head, and stitched that wound, no anesthetic! It sure did hurt, but no sound came out of my mouth as old Doc put three stitches into my head.

He finished, washed his instruments, put them back into his bag, looked at me and said, "You'll live." Amidst the goodbyes and "thank you very much," Doc Pearson went out into the night.

Larry and Dave had stood by intently watching as did Norm, who had been chastised by Mom by this time. They also had made no sounds during this "surgery." I knew what had kept me silent. I would never let these guys see me cry over this; I would have died first. They stared at me in wonder even after Mom had left the kitchen because she couldn't bear to watch. I went to sleep victoriously that night -- pain and all.

All during this time, I had to get the cows each evening and continued my running as intently as the first time I had run. I ran through fields, farmland, woods, wherever I could. I therefore decided to try out for the seventh- and eighth-grade track team. I don't remember these times with pride because I had very little confidence in myself and not much encouragement in running. Although I could outlast anyone in running if the race was long enough, I didn't get much of a chance to do this. In those days it was felt that anything longer than a half mile was detrimental to our young bodies, so no one ever saw just what I could do until many years later. The good news was that because I was the best we had in the "distance," I gained enough self-confidence to continue running in high school.

My sense of competitiveness was always high. While I was running track, I was still playing softball with my brothers, trying as usual to outplay Norm. One time we were in the field playing to see who could hit the ball the highest and deepest. Norm and I took turns hitting and playing the outfield because the younger boys were too young for anything except chasing bloopers. I tried and tried with all that I had to slam that ball across the road, but I couldn't do it. It irked me to no end, especially when it was Norm's turn, that over the road the ball went, as easy as could be! He ran around the bases with a cocky smile on his face like "You can't even come close to this, Bob, old boy." I was so jealous.

There was never any jealousy or roughhousing with the younger boys as there was between Norm and me because of this constant competing with each other. All during my youth, I would come to the point that I would feel good about myself and think my brothers saw me in a fairly positive light, when my health would turn as quickly as the weather would change.

Once I was standing on the front porch, one summer August evening, watching the sky darken by the minute. My father, brothers, and I were closing barn doors and getting things put away for the upcoming storm. When I went back to the porch to watch the sky, the wind started kicking up the dust in the gravel driveway and I knew the pollen was being stirred also.

All of a sudden, I felt my bronchial tubes start to swell. Because I knew the scenario well, I was really frightened even though I had gone through this so many times before. I quickly went into the house to lay on the couch, trying to be as relaxed as I could. If I tried to fight what was happening to my body, it would just become worse. My tubes continued to close up until the air could barely get through.

That sensation of suffocation was horrifying, but I didn't want to call my parents. I told myself this would pass, that I wasn't a baby. The attack went on for several hours. Although my family was still outside, they knew what was happening. It was such a common occurrence, everyone was used to it. Mom came in and checked periodically, though, as mothers will do. After a couple of hours or so, I'd come out of it although there were times when I would have to be rushed to the doctor for an injection. Once again I felt inferior and such a weakling.

Those were the times that I would crave doing something, anything, that would show my family that I could do something special. I didn't know what I'd do, but something. I had this thought in back of my mind when I was looking at the pear trees in our front yard. "I'll bet Norm couldn't climb as high as I could."

These pear trees were as high as a two-story house. The limbs at the top were intertwining and big enough to hold my weight. I'd have a great time climbing the trees and felt like I was really something. I'd climb high and crawl from tree to tree, making my way through all four before climbing down to the ground. It was through this experience that I had a scare turn into a revelation for me regarding the wonder of my body.

When I had finished with the pear trees in front, I went to the other side of the house to the giant apple tree. I climbed all the way up and stood overlooking the farm, when all of a sudden, the branch I was standing on snapped. I was tumbling towards the ground, crashing through branches, when I reached out and caught fast another limb as I went by it. The scare passed when I realized what had just happened. I just stopped myself from getting seriously hurt from that fall! It was the neatest thing in the world. I thought, "I bet there weren't too many people who could have done that!" As I climbed down the remaining distance to the ground, I thought for the first time, "Maybe my body is special, yeah, maybe it really is!"

This new awareness of the wonder of my body, plus my adventuresome spirit, were all building upon each other, slowly for sure, but preparing me for the day when I was to push my body to be all that it could be.

I spoke a little bit about this to my grandfather, who listened attentively. He didn't say much but just smiled, and I guess it was at this time that he realized we were growing up. He wasn't one to speak deeply about personal matters, but would be more subtle about his belief in us boys.

One of the last times we were to vacation together two incidents showed his willingness to let us answer the call of our growing spirits.

My grandfather, Norman, my cousins Ted and Tom Metz, and I had driven to Yellowstone National Park. As we drove by a meadow, we noticed a herd of buffalo. One was lying down by itself. I was taking pictures and walked closer. Grandpa just watched as I practically got on top of that bull for a good shot. When I got back to the car, a park ranger came up and told Grandfather, "Don't let the boys go out into the field where there is a lone bull, they're mean when they're by themselves as a younger bull has run them off from the cows."

Grandpa just nodded, put his hand on my shoulder, not saying a word. I felt warmed by the fact that he didn't jump all over me. I guess we had both learned something new that day. We got back into the car to our next little adventure.

Quite a few miles after the buffalo incident, we noticed a bear ahead of us. We stopped and Ted and I left the car to take more pictures. Grandpa stayed in the car as the bear came toward me. Grandpa did "ask" if he thought we'd better get back into the car.

"No, I'm gonna take just one more," I said. The bear came within 20 yards of me; I snapped the picture and then ran around the other side of the car and quickly got in. The bear got up on Grandpa's side, staring him in the face. He slowly pulled the car away and the bear slipped off the door. At the hotel that night, the bear's footprint was on the car, muddy and hard.

Grandpa said, "Don't you dare wash that footprint off." And when we returned home, he told my parents how the bear print got on the car, but he told his own version.

After our summer vacation, I had my usual bout of allergies, but was able to begin my freshman year of school. It just so happened that the school initiated a new cross country program.

"This is for me," I thought. The distance was only two miles, and I knew I could do it easily because I had run that far on the farm. As always, I had to wait for the first frost to combat the residual allergies before I could do my best, but I began training with four other boys who were to make up our team.

Training was probably too strong a term in those days, because it consisted of leaving the school gym, running to a point on the road a mile away and returning to the gym. In those days, especially with a new team, it made sense that if we had a two-mile race, that's all we needed to train. It was fortunate for me, though, that I rode my bike to school, which, of course, helped in my training.

During the spring I was looking forward to track and field because I was now going to be able to run the mile instead of just 800 yards. As the season progressed, I continued to improve until I was closing in on a senior teammate. Although the times were not extraordinary, they were competitive for our area. He was running about 5:15 and I was just a few seconds back with the league meet in one week.

A good mental attitude is so important in trying to be the best -- AND THAT'S WHAT I WANTED TO BE, THE BEST -- and I visualized staying close to him and beating him at the finish. Was I excited!

Friday finally arrived, and we were in the small town of Trotwood, near Dayton, and would be running on a cinder track under the lights. I loved doing that. I jogged easily for ten minutes before they called us to the line. I didn't want to overdo it, (In my naivete, I didn't realize the body needed more than that before it was ready to compete.) Because this was really tough competition, my coach's dream was that one of us would at least place and, of course, he was counting on Ron King.

Here we were, about twelve of us, and my intent was to beat my teammate; nothing else mattered. (Misdirected thoughts they were, but I was young and have no other excuse.) The gun sounded and we were off. The better runners went into the lead and I settled into ninth or tenth place. My teammate, Ron, was a few places in front.

After the first lap, I passed one boy and then another; and then, there was Ron, right in front of me. I was feeling good and decided to pass him. As I moved up alongside him and then passed him, I was elated. I was in sixth place, just what the coach wanted. Because it was obvious I wasn't going to pass anyone else, all I thought about was holding my position. Confident and happy, I did indeed place sixth. What a thrill! I'd done it! I turned to see how far I had beaten Ron. I waited until everyone had finished. Where was Ron? I wondered what was going on. I asked one of my teammates. He replied, "Ron dropped out of the race."

I was furious. How could he? Why in the world had he done that? I found out later that he had problems with his breathing. I was even more furious. Never in all the training had he ever mentioned having a breathing problem, although everyone knew I had this problem. Then I thought how selfish that sounded. As difficult as it was, I had to let it go. Because my time was faster than he had ever run, 5:10, I knew I had beaten him. It was a little hollow, though, because he had dropped out.

Nevertheless, I chose to be positive and tried to look forward to the following year. As a sophomore I was the leader on the cross country team and the top miler in track, running 4:50. The mile was the longest distance they had.

Although I was still the top distance runner my junior and senior years, there was a fine half-miler, Ron Peele, who would win the state title his last two years. We were always trying to outdo each other and when we ran the mile relay, it was always a fight to see who would have the best time. Usually both of us would run .51+ for our leg of the relay but he would usually have the faster split.

In my junior year, I ran 4:34.4 for the mile and ended up making it to state, even though I had not yet learned to push my body, nor yet learned the enormous concentration necessary to become a great runner. My parents and brother Dave were there at state, and at least I was feeling better about myself. I was giving them something about me in which to be proud, for it was no shameful thing to come in fifth. In my senior year I ran almost exactly the same time and ended up in fifth again. My highest cross country state finish was seventh my senior year.

Ron was offered a scholarship at Ohio State. One summer day Ron and I were on his front porch visiting, when Ohio State's head coach pulled up in his car and approached Ronnie. Coach Larry Snyder wanted a private talk with Ron. Ron resisted because I was there but the coach's words were: "Bob won't mind." I was so hurt and angry as the coach put his arm around Ron, led him to his car, and drove away. I felt so insignificant.

As I rode my bike home, many thoughts came to me. The coach's aloofness toward me was like a slap in the face. I felt I wasn't the quality he wanted. Ronnie was much deserving of this attention, I knew, but the anger I had was toward myself. I had not performed as well as I could have. I wanted the same fruits Ron had. I was humiliated at being shoved aside so easily and was so glad no one was there to see me like this. I knew then I was going to do my best at becoming a better runner and that one day I would also become worthy of this attention.

After my senior year of high school, I decided to work a year before going to school. I hadn't received any notification for scholarships at Miami University, or anywhere else, and wanted to work my own way through college. Then I received a phone call from Miami Coach George Rider, just four days before the start of school.

He said he had some financial aid left over and that he could give it to me. I made a quick decision. I still remember it vividly as I said, "it is too late," I had made up my mind to work a year before going to school, and within seconds, I refused him. Because of my immaturity in handling this gift, my first reaction was to turn it down. When I hung up the phone, my heart sank. I shouldn't have said no, yet I didn't know how to undo it. I went to my room and looked out the window for a long time. Then, as before, I had to let it go. I sighed, went downstairs to talk with my father, who then made arrangements for me to work at Frigidaire, a division of General Motors in Dayton. The year was a long one and I was very happy when the following September rolled around.

By the time I arrived at Miami University to join Norm, who was a senior, I was very enthused about it all. Norm was going to graduate in just three years due to his high academic standing, whereas I, although among the top 10 percent in high school, rarely studied. My bad study habits had unfortunately carried over to college. I had to develop new habits very quickly if I wanted to pursue my running career under George Rider. He had the reputation of turning out some of the best distance runners in the Midwest.

After settling in to the dorms, I went over to the physical education building to look for Coach Rider. I was in luck. The team was gathered in back of the building, getting ready to work out. I approached Coach Rider and blurted out, "My name is Bob Schul and I'd like to try out for the cross country team."

He was taken aback as he looked at me. Obviously, all the athletes here had been recruited, and I must have sounded egotistical with this statement. The athletes looked at me, and in this "pause," I felt embarrassed. The coach stood there for what seemed like forever, his hand going through his white hair as if he were thinking.

He looked so strong for a man in his early 60s; he had obviously kept himself in good shape. "Bob Schul," he said in a quizzical sort of way. "Aren't you the fella from Milton Union? I offered you a partial scholarship last year?"

I nodded my head as I said, "Yes, sir." His hand was on his chin now as he processed my credentials. "4:34, right?"

"Yes, sir!" I answered, impressed that he knew this. Then putting the record straight, I said, "4:34.4 to be exact."

"Oh, yes, 4:34.4," he said, grinning. I felt stupid for being so exact, but then he reached down and grabbed my hand and almost shook my arm off. "Boys, come over here; I want you to meet the newest member of our team." I was introduced to everyone and even knew some of the athletes since I had run against them.

Over the next few days Coach Rider and the runners really made me feel like part of the team. Well, here I was on the team even after turning down that scholarship last year. I guess I'm like my father in the sense that he didn't mourn or have regrets over the past; he just moved on.

In the years to come I found George Rider to be a person who exemplified everything that had ever been written about a teacher in athletics. He not only knew what had to be done in training an athlete, but he was like a second father and good friend as well. Very seldom would he become angry, and even then it was subdued. He never cursed and the strongest phrase I ever heard him use was, "He's a double Jackass!" He never smoked, didn't believe in drinking, and would have no qualms about kicking a boy off the team if he was seen doing either. He was a man of principle, and no matter what the consequences might have been to him or the team, he never bent.

There was such a profound respect between the coach and runners due to his going the "extra mile" with us. In bad weather, during January and February, he would stand in the cold, bundled up in a heavy top coat, thick scarf and galoshes over his shoes, constantly encouraging us. In between workouts, he'd talk about the aspirations he had for us as runners. When he spoke of these things he spoke from the heart, knowing our potential and wanting the best for us. He knew we could do it, and when he spoke he could see these dreams visualized. We could, too.

There isn't any particular incident to tell of the greatness of this man. His way of life was his greatness. In addition to his positive qualities, he had a tremendous amount of knowledge, psychologically as well as physically. It was because of this deep respect, which I need to restate, that we wanted to reach our potential, not only for ourselves but for him.

Coach Rider had a lot of patience with me because I had a slow start that fall. I had been out of competition for over a year and the pollen was still abundant. Our warm-up was more than I had ever done in a full workout in high school.

Coach Rider said in an interview that we were the best freshman team he had seen at Miami in 20 years. We may not have had the big stars, but we were balanced and as the season progressed, I continually improved until I was challenging for first-place honors.

The experience was interesting. As a walk-on I wasn't expected to run near the front, but eventually I did just that. I began to ask myself why I was running better than the others when we were basically doing the same things in workouts. All my teammates looked smooth when they ran, and I didn't feel that way at all. Why was I able to beat them?

I assumed in those days everyone pushed their body equally. Fatigue came to everyone in equal amounts. If that was true, then something else was happening inside that enabled me to run faster. I didn't concern myself with what was happening. I was happy with progressing and would leave this mystery to Coach Rider.

After the season ended, Coach Rider convinced me it would be best if I continued running throughout the winter. I had never trained in the winter before and wondered where that could be done. I didn't need to worry, for Coach Rider had found a winter training area many years before. When the snows became too deep to run on the grass, we went to the roads. There wasn't a nice warm indoor facility. If there had been a snowfall he had the maintenance crews clear one stretch of road near the freshman dormitories. He had every distance from 220 yards to one mile marked on the roads and every day, unless the weather was exceptionally bad, we would train.

We trained in our warm-up suits with several layers underneath, along with a knit cap and gloves. (No polypropylene and nylon wind breakers.) Our sweats were mostly heavy, bulky cotton. You'd think this dress would help us become better runners. But I'm not so sure as movement was thwarted and it was a struggle to run with all that weight.

During the winter we ran uneventful freshman relays intermixed with varsity events. It was great when the warmer days took the last of the snow away and we could use the track once again.

That spring was an unusual one for me. On the freshman team, I was pressed into running the 4 x 220, the 4 x 440, and the open 440 because I had more speed than the other distance runners and we needed an extra man in those events. It was a lot of fun even though I didn't do well but these races were teaching me to relax while I ran. In later years this would prove to be an advantage.

I returned home for the summer and led a quiet life helping my parents. I also was a lifeguard at Miller's Grove swimming pool, ten miles away. I had not yet learned that year-round training was necessary to be successful. I put running plans away for the summer.

In the fall my family wished me well as I returned to Miami. I began training anew, anxiously looking forward to the first frost and the end of hay fever season. This came about at the end of September and my races improved until the temperatures dropped below 40 degrees. At that point, the cold air gave me problems with asthma. Nevertheless, I was progressing; training with the added handicap of these physical problems allowed me to place more stress on my body than others. I was elated as my health improved, I was getting closer to our top man, Dick Clevenger, one of the best distance runners in the Eastern part of the United States.

Before college the last time I ran against Dick was as a junior in high school, when he whipped me soundly every time. Now in the Mid-American conference championships, I caught up with him at the last 440 in the race and we ran in together. I didn't want to pass him as he was a hero to me and now was not the time to beat him, if I could. He would have fought me every step of the way if I had tried and as it was we were not going to gain or lose a position. Our second- and third-place positions did us no good, however, because the rest of the team was far back. Miami lost its first Mid-American championship in the history of the meet.

November 24, 1957 was the first time in a major meet for me. It was the NCAA cross country championship, one in which I could observe some truly great American and foreign distance runners. Among them was the eventual winner, Max Truex of the University of Southern California. It was hard to believe an athlete so short, 5 feet, 1 inch, and so stocky, could be such a fine runner. I placed 20th, and was far back of the "Flying" Truex. (I had no idea that one day Max would become my good friend.)

The indoor season came and went with me having good success. My 440 time in the relay was under 50 seconds and I was looking forward to the spring outdoor races. I was to move up to the 880 and the mile. Again, I was matched against Clevenger, still the best of the distance men who ran the mile and the two-mile. He had beaten me in the early meets and now he was going to try for the school record against Ohio University.

The day was warm and beautiful as only the early part of May can be. As we prepared for the mile, Coach Rider called Dick over to have a last-minute word with him. I was taking off my sweats and overheard Coach telling him how to run the race.

"Dick, you're going to have to take the lead immediately, because there's no one else who's capable of going out as fast as you'll have to go. To break the record of 4:16, you need to run the first 880 in 2:06."

"All right, Coach," Dick replied, "I'll do my best."

As I thought about what Coach Rider had said, I knew I'd be able to stay with Dick for at least the 880, for my best time was 1:56, and 2:06 shouldn't be a problem. The only problem was his strength, which had allowed him to pull away from me in earlier races. I stayed with him for only three laps during those times, but now I felt in much better shape.

Dick was on pace and I was only a step back at the 880. The rest of the field had dropped back and wasn't in contention as we came to the end of the third lap.

"Right on, Dick!" Coach shouted. "Give it all you've got!"

Down the back straight I was still just a step behind. Could I hang on? I started thinking I might have a chance to win. The pace hadn't slowed as we came around the final turn and with each step I drew closer to Dick. With 50 yards to go we were even; we inched closer and closer to the tape. When Dick tired near the end, I edged ahead and beat him by one-tenth of a second. I was elated. The time was 4:14.4, and I now held the mile record for Miami University!

Although it was evident that Dick was disappointed, especially with his leading the race from the beginning with me hanging on, he was the first to congratulate me along with coach Rider. There were no hard feelings and their praise truly meant a lot to me.

As life would have it, glory is sometimes short lived. The next weekend, although lowering my time to 4:12.1, I was defeated by Western Michigan runner Art Eversole, who beat me by one tenth of a second, the same amount of time I had beaten Dick. I had to content myself with knowing I was becoming a better runner and thought I'd soon be able to run against the top collegians.

The NCAA championships were approaching and I was anxious to go to the West Coast to compete. At the last moment, though, the school decided they couldn't afford to send more than one runner, and of course, that was Dick Clevenger, the senior. I was deeply disappointed that I couldn't join Dick out West, but I realized something profound: for me to be that disappointed meant my confidence had increased tremendously.

My sophomore year ended and my summer was spent at school. For the first time, I continued to train hard until the hay fever season was in full swing. Then I had to lighten my load because of breathing problems. But with only eight weeks of lighter training, I came back that fall in better shape than ever before. From the beginning I was leading the team and we had a fairly successful season. I was feeling good about everything and wasn't prepared for the tragedy that soon entered my life.

There was a knock on my dorm room door. "What is it?" I shouted.

"Phone call downstairs."

Who'd be calling me at this hour, I thought? I made my way down the steps to the first floor and reached the booth.

"Hello?"

"Bob, I have some bad news."

The voice on the phone was my mother's and I didn't ever remember hearing her sound like this, something was terribly wrong, I thought.

"What is it, Mom?" I asked.

She told me the story.

Tom Metz, my first cousin, was returning to Florida State. My brother Dave, who had just turned 16, was going to drive with my grandfather and Tom to Florida. Dave had taken the wheel after lunch and my grandfather had stretched out in the back seat to take a nap. Because they were going to be driving late into the night, Tom had dozed off in the passenger seat, his knees against the dash.

Dave was very cautious on this hilly highway, but was making good time. On every hill there was a third lane used as a passing lane for those cars needing to pass slow vehicles. Dave was nearing a curve and the road ahead was not yet in view. As he approached the curve and started down the hill, he viewed a scene that made his blood run cold: coming at him was a car that was passing another vehicle.

The passing lane had ended but here was this car still trying to pass another. There was nowhere to go. To the right was a 500-foot drop and to the left were the two cars and a steep hill. His foot instinctively went to the brake, but there was no time to slow. The head-on collision brought both cars to a stop within seconds; twisted metal, shattered glass, radiators sending up steam amidst screams from the cars. And then a second collision as the car following Dave couldn't stop in time and rammed into this horror. With no seat belts, bodies were thrown around the car interior. Tom flew into the windshield, Dave's knees went into the dashboard, his face hitting something, his teeth going through his lips. Only his hanging on to the steering wheel so tightly saved his life.

"Bob, the boys are in the hospital, but Grandpa was killed instantly." Her voice broke.

I couldn't speak. Tears were flowing down my face. She said they were going to Kentucky and would call me from there. I was in a daze. "Are you allright, Bob?"

I couldn't talk, as I was sobbing. I finally said, "I'm here, Mom. I'll hear from you in a couple of days then?"

"I'll call you as soon as we know anything," came the reply. "Good-bye, son."

"Bye, Mom."

I hung up the phone and made my way back to my room. I was glad my roommate was not there to see my distress. God, I loved my grandfather. Why did he have to be killed? The hours went by as I cried and thought about what had happened and in the early morning I fell into an exhausted sleep.

One of the most difficult things I've ever had to do was attend my grandfather's funeral. After it was over and I went back to school I didn't study any more. I had never taken the time to study properly and with my emotional attitude I knew there wasn't any sense in continuing. My semester grades were terrible as I expected and I decided to leave school.

TWO

Time To Grow Up

By the time I left college and joined the Air Force in February 1959, I felt like my old self again. I was content to be going to Texas and basic training, spending six weeks learning military life. Thirty of us who were in electronics and had scored high in math on our entrance exams were to be shipped out early to a training school at Keesler Air Force Base, Miss. After arriving at Keesler we found ourselves going to school from 6 p.m. until midnight and eating dinner after we returned from school. This gave us about a 2 a.m. bedtime each morning. It was not a fun time.

One day as I passed a bulletin board, a notice caught my eye. An Air Force championship track and field meet was to be held in Denver, and everyone on the base was eligible to try out for the team. It looked good to me. Life was too boring here and I needed to get back into training, which I started right away.

After getting to bed at 2 a.m., I'd awaken at 7 a.m., and go to the track located on the base. I'd work out for only an hour. It was very tiring, but I worked hard for the next couple of weeks. It paid off when I found out I was chosen for the Air Training Command team. I had qualified with a time of 4:30 for the mile and close to 15 minutes for the three-mile.

Denver was a beautiful city, full of good, clean air. It was also full of competition, which would be more difficult than it had been on base. During the next two days, I ran against Bill Dellinger, who was more competition than I could handle. I placed second in the three-mile and third behind Dellinger and Larry Means in the mile. Bill also won the steeplechase. Dellinger was so far ahead in all three races it wasn't even a contest.

Because we were leaving the next afternoon for Mississippi, I wanted to run in the morning. As I was cooling down in the infield, I overheard Dellinger talking with Jim Bailey, the man who had defeated the great Australian, John Landy, in a mile race in Los Angeles. They also were planning to run in the morning and I was excited at the prospect of running with them. I mustered up the nerve to approach them.

"Lieutenant," I began, "if you're going for a run in the morning, could I join you?"

They both looked at me with expressions that were almost blank. There was a slight pause and then Bill said, "Well, we're going pretty early in the morning and we'll be doing a fast run."

With that he turned away and I felt embarrassed. I walked away, disheartened, trying to understand their rebuff. After my morning run I packed for the trip back to Mississippi and decided to forget about training. It was time to buckle down and learn as much about electronics as I could.

As the months passed we became well versed in the jobs we'd be doing for the next three and a half years. In November we received our assignments and I was slated to go to Selfridge Air Force Base, north of Detroit. I had hoped to go to California because most of the competition was on the West Coast. In 1959 there just weren't many races for non-collegiate athletes, and I figured my running career was finished before it had even begun.

After I arrived in Michigan and had settled in, I wanted to start training for physical fitness. Snow was already on the ground and it was impossible to run outside. I found a small gym on the base and jogged around its basketball court. It was boring and hard on the ankles if I went too fast, so my pace was fairly slow.

The months went by and I was working with the aircraft electronic equipment. It was terribly cold on the flight line working on those planes. The temperature was below zero, but even so, we would occasionally work without gloves. We had to be very careful, for if we left our hands on the aircraft too long, they would just stick there.

Some time later in the gym I saw a notice on the bulletin board. As I read it my heart started to pound. Maybe my career in competition running wasn't over after all. The notice asked for any track athlete to apply for special training for the Air Force track team, and it was apparent they didn't want just anyone.

The team selected would be in training for the Olympic Trials for the 1960 games in Rome, Italy. At the bottom of the page were listed various times for each event. I didn't qualify for any of them; a feeling of remorse came over me. I only had a 4:12 in the mile whereas a 4:09 was specified. I thought about it, took a deep breath and decided to apply anyway.

The article requested press clippings, so I called my parents, who had fully accepted my new life in the Air Force and were very supportive of me. They mailed the clippings to me and I wrote the necessary letter that I hoped would enable me to renew my competitive spirit and to leave this cold weather.

Weeks went by and still no word. Every time I went to the mail room I could feel the adrenaline flowing as I worked the combination on my mail box. Finally, after I had almost given up hope, I received a letter from the Air Defense Command in Denver. I opened the letter slowly as I envisioned what it would say. It was frightening as I started to read:

"Airman Schul," it began, "your times do not qualify you for special training for the Air Force team." I almost stopped reading as the news couldn't get any worse. Then the second paragraph started: "However, Airman Schul, we have decided your various marks are good enough for you to be part of the Air Defense team."

My emotions soared from rock-bottom to tremendous elation! What a feeling came over me. The letter went on to tell me orders were being "cut" immediately in Denver and were being sent to Selfridge. The new assignment would be Oxnard Air Force Base in California, 60 miles north of Los Angeles. I was elated. Yes!

A few days later I received a call from the processing office.

"You're being transferred to California," the sergeant stated.

"Oh, really," I said matter of factly, "When do I leave?" Inside, my heart was doing cartwheels.

"Right away."

It would take me a day to take care of everything I had to do, such as receiving travel money and turning in the various items of equipment and bedding. It was a joyful day as I made my rounds, and even the cold weather didn't seem so bad.

I kept my bedding for one more night and early the next morning I turned it in, packed my English MG for the trip to a new adventure, and off I went. Three days later I crossed over into California and the warm weather of the West Coast made my spirits rise even more.

When I arrived at Oxnard, I found to my surprise that the team selected to train for the U. S. Olympic trials was also training there and I'd be allowed to join in their training sessions. God was surely looking over my shoulder.

During the practice session the next day I found the Air Force could field a good team, for among the members were runners such as Eddie Southern, second best 440 hurdler in the U. S., and Max Truex, the nation's best distance runner. It was a pleasure to be running again, and the bonus was that with the training for the Air Force competition, we didn't have any regular duties to perform

It wasn't long before Max was helping me in my workouts. Within a few weeks I was doing workouts that were harder than I had done in college. I was learning what it takes to become a top runner, as I observed and trained with Max in his workouts. With the warm weather and the training, I was feeling like my old self again. My racing times were becoming faster.

Max helped me join the Southern California Striders, which was *the* club in the United States, and I ran in several relays for them.

During the spring I ran my first two races in the steeplechase, but I knew nothing about the event and had never gone over the water-jump. The only hurdle training was with Eddie Southern, who showed me the proper hurdling techniques. I finished with a 10:45 at the Mt. San Antonio relays, and later I decreased my time to a 10:15 during the Air Force championships. Although they were slow times, to say the least, my ability and confidence were increasing with each race, I raced in the 1500 meter and was selected to be on the Air Force team to run in the U. S. championships.

Unfortunately, during the trials I wasn't concentrating very well because I was frightened. Although I finished fifth and failed to qualify for the finals, my time was 3:55, or approximately a 4:12 mile, which equaled my lifetime best. I was angry with myself for running such a poor tactical race. I have a lot of work to do, I thought, but was bolstered by the knowledge that I believed I could run close to the leaders. I just needed more experience and racing savvy. I believed in myself.

Included among the top four runners was a foreign athlete, Laszlo Tabori, who was being trained by the famous Hungarian, Mihaly Igloi. One day Laszlo would give me tremendous incentive that lasted throughout my career.

This was the end of the season for me and I returned to Oxnard finally having to go to my duty station. Luck was with me. My work shift was from 8 a.m. to 4:30 p.m., and the athletes who had qualified for the Olympic trials were training at 5 p.m. I was, therefore, able to continue training with them. I was so lucky to be in this position. Max would still give me the workouts, and even though I was training harder than ever before, I still couldn't manage his complete training schedule. Max had trained under Igloi for a short time before I'd arrived at the base, and Igloi was still guiding him. It was no surprise that during the Olympic trials, Max ran away with the 10,000 meters.

Now I was on my own. I used the training Max had given me, and was determined to be in even better shape when he returned from Rome. I realized it was the Igloi system, but didn't know how important it would become in my life.

Watching the results of the Olympics was very exciting that year. Max placed sixth in the 10,000 meters, breaking the American record. All the publicity said it was a breakthrough for the Americans, but the Europeans didn't seem to be impressed. We didn't care because Max had given many of us the incentive to train harder and wiser than we had ever done before. Maybe now someone could break into the European running monopoly.

Max toured Europe after the Olympic Games and didn't return until mid-September. The day after his arrival we were training together again. Larry Means, who was my commanding officer, and Eddie Southern, who had won the silver medal in the 400-meter hurdles, joined us. Although the three of them were officers, and I was a lowly airman, it was never mentioned. I was made to feel part of the group.

I began to realize what it meant to train with a group of talented athletes who were so dedicated to running. They helped me tremendously by drawing upon each other's energy. I looked forward to the workouts, even though my body was rebelling. I thought again of falling from that tree as a child, catching myself, and marveling at the wonder of my body. It didn't matter what my body was doing, I was in charge.

That autumn was a lot of fun as we left the track. There was a golf course nearby with some very long and steep hills. It was a beautiful place to train, and the course was never crowded when we trained so we didn't have many problems with the golfers.

After warming up we would find a flat area and do some repeats, then jog on the course until we came to another flat area. We never measured the distances, but would run from tree to tree. Southern would always leave us behind if the distances were short, but the advantage would go to someone else as the distance increased.

Although Means was a capable runner, he didn't have the talent of Truex or Southern, and I was beginning to catch up with him as my body progressed. He was the extrovert of the group and would keep our spirits high with his stories and playfulness.

At least once a week Means would challenge the rest of us to a race up a steep hill at the end of a workout. I don't know if he had loafed on the other part of the workout or not so he'd be ready for this challenge, but he would goad us into accepting. Off we'd go with Southern in the lead, Means in second, Truex in third, and then me.

Depending on the hill, there was a time when Southern would begin to slow and the rest of us would overtake him. Then, depending on the day, it was a race to the top. Larry seldom won the race and would always state, during gasps for air and his hands on his knees, "Damn you guys -- next week I'm going to beat your ass!" Truex and I would just smile as we looked at each other, and Southern wouldn't say a word as he lay on his back heaving from exhaustion.

On other days we would go to the beach on the Pacific ocean. After a warm-up of two or three miles we'd do our intervals in the hard sand next to the water. Then Larry would get the bright idea of playing follow the leader. He always became the leader for the first go-around, and he'd set off with the rest of us in single file.

You couldn't pass until someone had dropped back several yards, but it wasn't long before Southern was last. No matter who had the lead, we'd run along the hard sand and then suddenly turn and head into a sand dune. The soft sand was very difficult in which to run and very tiring. Then back again into the water, where we'd have to lift our knees high. Back and forth we'd go until we were completely exhausted. We'd all end up gasping and cursing Larry for initiating the torture. It wasn't long before we were recovered enough to begin again, and someone else would become the leader.

An interesting thing was beginning to happen. As the fall months continued, I could sometimes pull away from Truex when I was leading. I couldn't have done that a few months before. With the confidence I had gained, I realized my body was becoming a better machine. There was no doubt I was gaining on Truex, although I knew I had to do a lot of training before I could be his equal.

The winter had been a fun and beneficial time for me. I was in a few relays with Southern and two other athletes. It wasn't a bad team and I contributed my part. In a few of the meets, I also ran the mile; but my best finish in the event was a third place at the Portland, Ore. Invitational.

I was beginning to think I could run with the top people in the United States. Max must have noticed my increasing potential also, for he came to me with the suggestion I try to train under Igloi, with whom he would request a month's training. He'd then try to arrange temporary duty in San Jose for the express purpose of training. Within a few days Max told me Igloi had agreed. All we had to do now was convince the Brass that it was a good idea.

Somehow Max persuaded the Air Defense Headquarters I should go, but only for two weeks. They arranged the temporary duty for May; and since it was only March, I'd have two months of training in addition to local competition before I would travel to San Jose.

Since I had some success in the steeplechase the year before, I decided to keep after it. Eddie Southern, a graduate of the University of Texas, arranged for me to attend the Texas relays in April and I flew down with him to compete. That was a wonderful experience, for he was a hero throughout the city. We were met at the airport by a resident assigned to pick us up.

"Eddie, it's a pleasure to have you back," said the driver.

"Thanks, it's always great to come home," Eddie said, smiling

After settling in at our motel, we went to the stadium. Just walking into the huge structure excited me. Tomorrow I'd be running in front of thousands of people. I was feeling great. After we left the stadium and had walked several blocks, we heard a shout from across the street.

"Eddie! Eddie Southern!"

We both stopped and turned to see a barber running out of his shop toward us.

"Eddie, how are you!" the barber asked as he enthusiastically extended his hand.

Eddie grasped his hand and they chatted for a minute like long-lost friends. I could see into the window of the barbershop that a customer sat waiting, fully lathered. Finally the barber excused himself and with a wave, disappeared into his shop.

"Who was that?" I asked, expecting the answer to be Eddie's personal barber.

"I don't know." Eddie replied, "Probably a Longhorn fan."

Before we left that section of town, we were stopped several more times. Each time it was the same. Eddie didn't really know the people, but he was nice enough to chat with them. Eddie was that type of guy. He was nice to everyone, making it no coincidence that so many people in this college town thought so highly of him.

The next morning I awoke very excited and wiled away the hours after our morning run with television and the day's paper. About noon we went to the stadium; Eddie was to run at 1:30 p.m.

I relaxed as Eddie talked with many officials. I knew it was going to be tough for him to run a good race without being able to concentrate more fully. At about the same time Eddie was called to the starting line, it was time for me to warm up. I watched him compete as I jogged easily at the end of the track. Eddie finished second to Ohio State's Glenn Davis, who had won the gold medal in the Rome Olympics where Eddie had won the silver.

My race wasn't spectacular. Once again I was frightened and didn't really get going, but I did finish third and was getting better at judging the barriers. My time was a personal best of 9:36, and I knew I could go faster.

Emotions play such an important part in racing, and I knew if I was to compete on an equal par with the best in the world I'd have to learn how to keep my emotions in check until the right time. Each race taught me a little more, and I was finally accepting a way of thinking that would help me throughout my racing career.

In essence, that was to accept the fact that I would only run as fast as I had prepared my mind and body. The trick was to bring myself to the starting line under control. I couldn't worry about what hadn't happened. This entire process wasn't easy, and I was constantly bringing into my thoughts all types of scenarios that would confuse my state of mind. I hoped one day to be able to control my mind, so I would be completely at ease, or at least close to it.

I realized, however, since emotion could be very helpful in bringing the body to its zenith, I'd have to use it during the race. By releasing the adrenaline, and possibly other hormones in the body, I'd be able to give my body strength that otherwise wouldn't be there. Therefore, I'd have to learn the trick of building emotion at the right time.

After that race, I was accepted to compete in the Mt. San Antonio College relays in California and this time I won with another personal best of 9:14.7. I had really improved but again realized I wasn't running to my ability. I was, however, gaining even more in confidence.

The weeks passed quickly, and I was on my way to San Jose to train under the great Igloi. There was no denying that I was excited -- very excited!

It was a bright spring day when I arrived on the field and saw a group of athletes together, so I walked over and asked them where I could find Coach Igloi. They pointed to the other side of the track. "Over there." I could see another group of athletes talking with an older man. As I walked over to him, other athletes were congregating in the same area, chatting and joking with one another. I finally got my break and boldly blurted out,

"Coach Igloi, I'm Bob Schul, and Max Truex made arrangements for me to train with you.

"You are who?" Igloi asked, in very broken English.

"Bob Schul. I'm in the Air Force with Max Truex."

"Ah, yes," he said. "Now I remember; Max told me about you." At that point he turned away and spoke to the other runners in his halting English, telling them to begin their warm-up. He then turned back to me.

"So. You want to train with me and my boys."

"Yes, sir," I replied. "Max thought it would do me a lot of good."

With that he gave a broad smile and ran both hands through his gray hair, which was combed straight back in a typical European style.

"So, you think you can train with my runners?" he asked.

"Yes, sir. I've been training under Max's instructions, and I think I'm in good shape. Max told me about your workouts, and I want to do them. I know I can do anything you ask of me."

Igloi paused and then looked at me with a slight smile. "Today you will only watch," Igloi said. "Tomorrow morning you will begin to train."

I almost ate those words during the next two weeks, for it was more work than I had ever dreamed possible the human body could endure.

I watched his athletes that afternoon during a three-hour workout. I'd never seen any athlete go through the work I saw that day. Twice-a-day workouts were not usually done under Igloi for newcomers, but when I told him I only had two weeks before the Air Force championships, he allowed the two sessions to begin.

I called home that night, keeping in touch with my family and letting them know I'd begun my training with Igloi. Although they weren't knowledgeable about Igloi's reputation, my excitement about him was enough for them to be happy for me. Mom, of course, was concerned about where I'd be staying since I was only in San Jose for two weeks. I assured her I was well taken care of. It might have been a slight exaggeration.

That evening I bedded down with a group of bachelors and slept on their couch. It had to have been through the Salvation Army at least twice, I'm sure. I tossed and turned and couldn't find a smooth place to rest on that ragged dilapidated thing.

I awoke very tired the next morning, but arrived at the track about 6:30 a.m. and found some of the runners already finishing their workouts. They were the ones who had to be at work by 7:30 a.m. Fortunately, there were a few who had arrived about the same time as I, and were warming up. Igloi said hello and told me to jog three laps. When I finished, there were two other runners waiting for me with Igloi.

"You can run with these boys," he said.

With that they turned and started jogging. I looked at Igloi, not sure if he meant me, too. He saw the confusion in my eyes and said, "Go with them."

When I caught up with them, they informed me the morning workout was going to be easy because of the tremendous workout the night before. For the next hour we circled the inside of the track on the grass doing "fresh" to "good" speed for 100 and 150 yards. These were terms Max Truex had used when he'd given me workouts, so Igloi's words were not entirely new. "Fresh" speed meant the body was not under tension but you were still moving right along. "Good" was a step up, with a slight tension on the upper body.

We reported back to Igloi after we'd finished and he told us we were done. I would later learn this was a standard workout, but the pace would increase along with the number of repetitions. That same afternoon, however, was a different story.

As I warmed up with the rest of the runners, about 35 in all, I felt good and thought this wasn't going to be so tough after all. When we'd finished the two miles, we stretched as Igloi divided the runners into various groups. Finally there were just two of us remaining. I knew who he was; everyone did: the great Laszlo Tabori who had fled Hungary at the same time as Igloi. He had held the world record for 1500 meters. I felt honored being there with him.

As I waited, Tabori spoke with Igloi in their native tongue. Every so often Laszlo would look around at me and I could tell something was wrong. I felt very uncomfortable. After gesturing and loud voices, Laszlo turned and started to jog away. I stood looking at Igloi.

"Go with him" he said, and pointed in the direction of the retreating Tabori.

I moved away and quickly caught up to him.

"I'm supposed to run with you." I said to Tabori.

"Yes, I know," he answered with a coolness that was cutting.

"What are we going to do?" I asked. There was a pause as he stared at me.

"Just follow me." he replied, his voice rising slightly with signs of irritation.

Within a few strides we were into the first set. I tried to follow as closely to his shoulder as possible. Within 15 minutes he said, "That is all for now; two laps, jog."

With that he started easily around the track at a relaxed pace. Within minutes we were back to Igloi and again the conversation was in Hungarian. Again Laszlo started jogging away and Igloi motioned for me to follow. Wanting to know just how much energy I'd be needing, because I was worried I wouldn't be able to finish, I once again asked Tabori what we were going to do.

"Just follow me," Tabori said impatiently with a slightly raised voice.

Again we started, and this time it was harder with less of an interval. It was much more tiring than the first set, and I was glad when it was finished We jogged two laps and were then back to Igloi. Once again, another conversation I could not understand and Laszlo jogged away. I didn't wait to be given instructions this time, but followed him out again. He surprised me saying, "We are going to do 10 times 330 yards, one fresh and one good buildup."

With my previous concern at wanting to know how much energy I would need, I was almost sorry he told me, because now I really thought I couldn't stay up. As tough as it was, though, I did stay with him and through the next set as well. Finally two hours had passed, and Igloi gave the welcome word. "Finis!"

"You did well," said Laszlo.

I felt happy at his remark but could barely smile as we headed into the warm-down phase of the workout, 10 times 100 meters.

Everyone else was finishing now and joining us in the 100's. The joking and laughter started, but I was too tired to participate. It was a welcome respite, though, from the quasi-drudgery I had just gone through: two hours for the main workout and another hour for the warm-up and cool-down.

I finished up, not knowing the impact that Tabori would have on me. The incentives had always been there for me because I wanted to be the best and loved the notoriety. Also, to see my name in print was enough to keep me training hard and regularly. But in order for me to run my absolute best, it was important that I feel inspired. Here was the man who was to be that inspiration in the weeks and years to come.

I didn't know it that afternoon, but here was an athlete who would never give up and who would fight until I thought he would drop from sheer exhaustion. As I grew in strength and in character, I knew I wanted so much to emulate the great Laszlo Tabori.

As I found out in years to come, those first few weeks were my test. I watched Igloi examine each runner to find out if he'd fight when it was unbearable or if he'd give in to the pain and fatigue.

The next morning was the true start of that test. It happened that Tabori and I came to the track at the same time. What a better way to have me tested, although at the time I didn't understand what was going on. I was merely excited to run again with Laszlo. But this morning was different. It wasn't a game, it was a job.

When we had warmed up and returned to Igloi, the two Hungarians spoke in their native tongue. I saw Laszlo smile a few times during the conversation, but I didn't think anything of it. Soon Laszlo moved away from Igloi and motioned for me to follow him. When I excitedly asked him what we were going to do, his only comment was, "Do what I do."

After that he never said one word to me during the hour and a half workout, not even during the few slower recovery periods between the sets that Igloi had given him. Most of the period was spent sprinting up one side of the track and down the other. We ran 100 yards one time and 150 yards the next. After an hour, my body was devastated -- or at least I thought it was. Yet we continued, Laszlo running easily, sprinting with relaxation, while I fought to stay with him. Never had I been so tired. My mind reeled from the fatigue and the growing pain that accompanied it. Finally, it was over. Together we cooled down and only then did Laszlo talk. By then it wasn't important to me what he said. I hardly listened, but the lesson was clear. There was a time to work and a time to reflect on what you had done.

After changing my shoes I slowly walked to my car. I was beat. At the house where I was staying, a much nicer one than the night before, I lay down on the living room floor and could only stare at the ceiling. It was still early enough that a couple of the other boys hadn't yet gone to their jobs. Joe Douglas, who had originally rented the house, was eating a hurried breakfast so he could leave for his teaching job.

"Igloi a little rough on you this morning?" he asked between mouthfuls of cereal.

"I've never worked so hard in my life." I wearily answered. "Will it be this hard every day?"

Joe looked up from the table and a smile crossed his face. "No." he said. "Somedays will be much harder." With that he took his last bite and headed out the door. "See you round 4," he shouted over his shoulder.

"OK," was all I could muster as I continued to lie on the floor.

Within minutes all the other boys had left for their jobs, leaving me alone with the ceiling. I couldn't eat and I couldn't sleep. I was just too fatigued. As I looked at that ceiling, I wondered if I could make it; and, even more, I wondered if it would be worth all the pain. Finally, around noon, I pushed myself away from the floor and went to the kitchen for some food. I found some lunch meat and made a sandwich. Within ten minutes I was back on the floor again, trying to regain my strength.

It didn't seem very long before I heard a key in the lock, and as I glanced at the wall clock, I saw it was four in the afternoon. Joe Douglas came through the door and saw me lying where he'd left me earlier. He smiled again as he said, "Well, how did the day go? Did you get plenty of rest?"

Then he looked at me again, and with the same silly grin on his face said, "I see you got dressed early. That's what Igloi likes, athletes who are rarin' to go!"

I didn't say a thing.

Within 20 minutes all the other boys were home, preparing for their workouts. At 4:30 we picked up our spiked shoes and piled into one of the bigger cars, the five of us making our way to the San Jose State track for our session.

We arrived at the same time as many of the other athletes and we stood around talking until 5 p.m. Almost all of the athletes had taken jobs where they could make it to the track by 5 p.m., and many had sacrificed better paying jobs to do so.

At 5 p.m., without any urging from Igloi, we started to move around the track in a slow jog. We very seldom used the track proper, but the grassy area just inside.

Laszlo and another athlete, who was becoming one of the better U.S. distance runners from the mile through the three mile, led the group. He was Jim Beatty, and I'd come to know him as a dedicated and inspired athlete. It was apparent the two were the leaders of the entire group and I soon came to know what psychologists call the "pecking order." (I learned that on the farm a long time ago.) I was at the bottom now, and I wondered how long it would take before I could move up through the ranks.

After the two-mile jog, we spent a few minutes stretching while Igloi began calling runners and forming them into small groups. He gave them the first segment of the workout and off they went. This continued until everyone was gone except two of us; you guessed it, Tabori and me.

The scenario was the same. Soon Laszlo and I were driving ourselves around and around the track. I wasn't asking any questions now; I didn't want to know. Plus, I needed to save every last ounce of strength for the next time he'd shout, "Let's go!"

I didn't do everything Laszlo did that afternoon, for there was no way my body could have stood it. I was amazed at the amount of work he could do. I saw all the other athletes doing more than I had ever done. Igloi would pull me away from Laszlo for one set and while he had me do something easy, Laszlo would do something hard. Then again, we would be together, he leading while I pleaded with my body to respond. You can do it, you can do it, and I did. I had no recourse but to put my mind outside of my body emotionally, to detach it from my physical self. I had learned this profound secret.

The days rolled by and I no longer lay on the carpet all day. Oh, I was always tired during my short two-week stay with Igloi. But it was tolerable now. I was with Tabori for 80 to 90 percent of his workout, and I could see a change in his attitude toward me. The boys with whom I was living were becoming friendlier as the "outsider" was being welcomed into the family. Within a week I felt I had moved up in the pecking order, but knew I had a lot to prove before getting much further. I was going to make it; there was no question in my mind. After the second week, when it was time for me to leave, Igloi had a long talk with me.

"Bob," he said, "you have proven to me you can be a good runner. How long that will take, I am not sure. Can you come back here after the championships and train with me?"

I was so honored, yet disheartened when I had to reply, "Coach, I still have over two years left in the Air Force, and they'd never let me have temporary duty again for a long time. I don't know what will happen, but I thank you for the short time I've spent with you. I've never worked so hard in my life. When I get back, I'll try to continue this type of workout."

Igloi turned away briefly and it was a few minutes before he spoke again.

"You cannot," he said. "Do you think you can learn what it has taken me years to understand? It is not easy, this work." He continued, "Do you think Tabori and my other runners in Hungary could have held all the world records from 1500 through 10,000 meters without me? Look around you. Look at all my other boys. They are here because of me, and they are here because they want to be the best in the world. Only a few will be able to make it but here, with me, they will become the best runners they can possibly be."

It was quite a lecture. How could I explain that I didn't mean I could do it by myself. I felt upset and knew that somehow I'd have to make my way back to Igloi. "Coach," I said, "I want to train with you and I'll try to do just that."

How that would be possible I had no idea. My God! Here was the opportunity of a lifetime; but because I was in the Air Force, I would never be able to fulfill a dream that was beginning to form. There must be a way. Was it possible that if I trained under Igloi, I could possibly make the Olympic team? I thought if ever there was a time for making this happen, it was now. With training like this, I could become one of the best.

"Bob, I will give Max a workout and you can do the same thing until the Air Force championship," Igloi's voice interrupted my thoughts.

I was so grateful, I just shook his hand warmly and said, "Thank you, thank you so much."

With that I turned away and said good-bye to my new friends. I climbed into my car and drove back to the house. I showered and packed and was planning to leave early the next morning. It was Saturday night and the boys were going to have a party. They had invited about 20 people and their dates. Fortunately, they also invited some single girls they knew from their jobs.

Dating was something I was still shy about and really too busy with my running to get involved with, but I thoroughly enjoyed the camaraderie. That last evening was filled with laughter as we broke away from the training regimen.

Back at Oxnard I had only one week before leaving for the championships at Sheppard Air Force Base in Texas.

I ran the steeplechase, winning it in a slow 10:03.1 But by winning I moved on to the All-Service championships at Quantico, Va., where I was to run against the best steeplechasers in the United States, George Young and Charles "Deacon" Jones. I wasn't in their class, but because there were no other class runners in the other services I managed to place third, though I was quite far behind in 9:10.

The top three in all events were placed on the All-Service team, and we then ran in the national AAU championships the next weekend. These races were really United States championships because anyone who qualified was allowed to run, whether it be high school, college, the services, or a club runner. Up to now I didn't think I had a chance of doing well in the meet, but after checking the year's results I found my time in the All-Service meet was third in the nation. What a great feeling. I thought I was slow. I was still improving my technique and also my racing strategy with every race. During the week George and Deacon helped me on the technique of taking hurdles, and the "crash" course helped immensely.

This was to be my first real test in big competition. The day arrived for the meet and, again, I was scared. The night before Igloi had arrived with his top runners, including Beatty and Tabori. They helped me calm down and gain confidence as they were very sure of themselves, and it seemed to pass on to me. As it came time to warm up, I talked with Igloi, who encouraged me and said to run a "smart" race. In what seemed to be too short a time, the announcement came to report to the clerk.

During the race Young and Jones led the way. They had no other competition, and they fought back and forth, each trying to break away. The rest of us were 50 to 60 yards back in a small pack, trying to keep within shouting distance of them. With one lap to go, I was within a step of John Lawler, who had won the collegiate championships.

With 330 yards to go we were running side by side, and as we took the hurdle together, with 300 yards to go, we collided. Although we were both thrown off stride, I managed to regain my balance first, opening a five-yard lead. John never did recover his tempo and I knew I was going to place third as I pulled away from the others.

Over the last water-jump, I started to catch George and continued to close the gap until, at the tape, he beat me by 30 yards. It was not close, by any means, but it was much closer than it had been the week before. My time was 8:53.6. Deacon Jones won in 8:48, and George was second with 8:50.8.

Best of all, the three of us had broken the AAU meet record. I was ecstatic after the race and Igloi seemed as elated.

That night we celebrated by going to a Hungarian restaurant, eating goulash, drinking beer, and talking incessantly about the race. All of us talked about our own races, each other's races, and anybody else's races we could remember. Then things quieted down a bit as Igloi seriously pointed out where the tactics could have been better. Amidst the joy of the moment and the seriousness of the future, it was times like these when Igloi would reminisce about his past. He told us this story:

"I was officer in army for WW II, and that time the Germans they take Hungarians to fight on their side. We have to fight for Germans or be shot. I, Igloi, get taken by Russians. They put me in charge of prisoner camp because I was big officer.

"Each day Russians have Hungarians move pile of trees, their branches they were cut off, they were big trees, logs, 10 feet, 12 feet. Russians say, move logs to other end of camp. So every day, we move logs.

"But, one day (Igloi laughed and winked), I tell my men to move just one log to end of camp. Then, my men, me, we sit down at end of all these trees, these logs.

"Russian officer come say, 'Why you didn't move logs?' I look at him like he crazy and say, 'What, what you mean? My men, me, we work hard, very hard. You see, we have one more and that is all, then we done.' I look at him. He look at me very confessed, very confused. He then, he just go away."

We all laughed and looked at Igloi in awe for his great ingenuity. He then became serious again as he told us this was a good lesson in tactics and how important it was to always outmaneuver your opponent. How it was possible to have more respect for a man than we already did, I do not know, but we did. We held up our beer and toasted him.

This was to be the year we were to go to the Soviet Union for the annual dual meet. Only two men would be able to run against the Russians, and I was not included. Since we had four dual meets in European countries that summer, all in a short time, the AAU was pressured into taking a few extra runners. This would allow the other athletes to rest when the team ran against the weaker countries. Since I had run a respectable three-mile and had consistently brought my steeplechase time down during the year, I thought I had an even chance of going. Had it not been for Truex and Beatty, I wouldn't have been considered at all. They went to bat for me during the meeting when the AAU officials were doing the choosing. I sweated it out until Max came to tell me I had been chosen along with the miler, Jim Grelle. A happier athlete was not to be found! My first international trip. I hoped it would just be the beginning of a long line.

THREE

Moscow, 1961

When we landed in Moscow it was a different world, the world of the international athlete and a world I had dreamed about.

There was still work ahead. All the men who had been coached by Igloi trained together morning and night. Some of the coaches on the trip were amazed for they had never seen athletes train as we were training. The Igloi method, the idea of training twice a day with hard workouts both times, was being spread around. And it was different, using shorter, faster distances in the workouts. We were about to prove the United States could be competitive with the European powers in distance running.

I was not to take part in the Russian encounter, the first two finishers in the AAU meet would have that privilege. I watched excitedly as the United States men did well in all their events, up to and including the mile. After that, Truex was our only hope, and he made the Russians work for their victory. Tabori wasn't with us because he wasn't yet an American citizen; he had defected from Hungary during the Melbourne Olympic games in 1956 along with Igloi and more than 100 other Hungarian athletes in different sports.

The most vivid memory of the match with the Soviets was their walkers entering Lenin Stadium far ahead of their American rivals. To make matters worse, they were hardly sweating. As they entered, they took off the small caps used to keep the sun off their heads and twirled them on their fingers as the crowd went wild.

I thought it was an insult, as if some runner with a lap to go turned and motioned for his struggling opponent to hurry up and give him a race. I don't know if the Soviets meant anything by it, but I knew we had to improve in those weak events so it wouldn't happen again. We outscored the Soviets on the men's side, as was expected, for the United States had never lost a men's dual meet in the history of the sport. The women lost as was usual.

During our stay in Moscow we spent the afternoon walking the streets around Red Square. The people of the city stared at us as it was apparent we were foreigners because of the drastic difference in our clothing. The Muscovites wore drab colors that seemed to have been washed many times. Most of us wore very bright colors.

We had a few brief encounters such as the one when George Young and I were walking through the Square. A gentleman approached us and began talking in perfect English. He was short, about five feet tall, and told us he was a teacher from the Ukraine, in Moscow on vacation. His ancestry must been partially Mongolian for he had the look I had seen in textbooks.

He was very friendly and wanted our picture taken with him. Another U. S. athlete, who was close by, agreed to snap it for us. So with George on one side and I on the other, the picture was taken. As we chatted awhile longer, he told us film was very expensive, so he took pictures sparingly. Only very important shots were taken.

His monthly salary was less than George made in a week as a teacher. Of course, the cost of living had to be taken into account. I'm certain he didn't live at the standard of our American teachers. He told us many of the people in the streets were tourists, lining up for blocks to file past Lenin's tomb. We finally finished our interesting visit and said good-bye to this friendly Ukrainian.

Then we went to the Gum Department Store to see its various goods. Quite unlike an American store, there were separate shops, each with its own room, selling one particular item. After spending a couple of hours browsing through the different shops, buying a few items to take home, we returned to the hotel to get ready for the afternoon workout.

That evening we were going to take the subway to a huge recreational park in Moscow, which had a track. We must have looked strange to the people of Moscow in our brightly colored running clothing, as we rode the escalator to the underground train. That was an experience, for we continued going deeper into the earth. When we reached the bottom to board the train, we were three to four times deeper than the subways in New York City.

We were amazed at the cleanliness of the platforms and the absence of graffiti on the walls. Instead, the station platforms were very aesthetic, with murals of leading Soviet people on the walls. We found out later the subways had been constructed for possible bomb shelters.

We had been told what train to take and which stop was close to the recreational center, and it wasn't long before our arrival. As we entered the grounds and began jogging, we estimated the area to be 25 acres. We saw an ice skating stadium, a gymnastics building, two running tracks, and many recreational areas where the local populace could enjoy themselves. One particular activity interested me as I stopped to watch.

At one end of the area were wooden objects stacked on top of each other. It reminded me of the game at a county fair in which milk bottles were stacked in pyramid fashion, and people tried to knock them over with baseballs. Here, the men were throwing what reminded me of a small baseball bat, a cylindrical object. From 20 yards away they'd let this thing fly, and it would slam into the stacked wood, which would fly all over the place. Because skill is non-ethnic, like Americans, some were better than others, and many missed the stack altogether.

As we were moving away I noticed someone coming down the road and his movement was such I thought he must be on roller skates. As he passed I noticed they were skates alright but not the ordinary kind. These had all the wheels in a line like ice skates. What a novel idea.

On another day, as we were standing outside the hotel deciding the morning's plans, a group of four young Soviet teens passed by. I made a remark to George wondering if they could speak English. Without hesitation one of the students whirled about and assured us they could speak very good English. Apparently insulted, they spoke in a less than cordial tone.

Several days later, I was walking by myself, crossing Red Square, when a young man came up to me and asked in flawless English if we might talk. He said he was a university student and wanted to know all about my life: what I did, where I lived, if I owned anything that was exceptional. As we talked, it became evident that almost everything I owned was exceptional. He could hardly believe I owned a car, a television set, and various other items most Americans take for granted. We talked for more than 15 minutes. It was then time for me to return to the hotel. In saying good-bye, he asked if I would meet with him at the same location the next day to continue our talk, and I agreed. The same location meant we were in the middle of Red Square away from any buildings where someone might be listening.

The following day he was waiting for me when I arrived. We spoke only briefly before he asked if he could introduce me to someone. I agreed and he motioned to a girl standing 30 meters away who came running. He introduced me in an excited voice to his sister. We talked for several minutes as his sister listened. When we said good-bye, I realized that this chance meeting of new friends would have to last a lifetime.

The day after the meet we departed for West Germany, where I was entered in the steeplechase with Deacon Jones. This was to be my first international competition and I wanted to do well. As I warmed up I felt so good I knew I was going to run well.

From that day on, through all my competitions, I could predict how fast I would be capable of running. Although I wasn't always able to run to my ability, since many races were strategical, I always ran to win. If I lost, it was because another athlete had prepared better for the contest or had outmaneuvered me during the race. Even when I didn't win I never lost confidence in myself; I just analyzed why and tried to correct it.

As this race began, the German, Mueller, took the lead, and I followed in second. I allowed him to lead for about 300 yards, then decided to take over and up the tempo. I've always believed runners should run the way they feel and how their strengths measure up against their opponents. Many times I've led a race most of the way because I felt good out front. I led this race with Jones and Mueller on my shoulder. Up to the last water-jump and over it, I felt very strong. I thought I had the race won. I could see the finish tape as I approached the last barrier and I thought how great it would be to win my first international competition.

As I was in the air over the last hurdle with only 70 yards to the finish, someone flew by me. When I landed and started running again, Deacon Jones was three yards in front and sprinting. I started after him and began to close the gap ever so slightly. Closer and closer I came to his shoulder as we approached the finish. We both dove for the tape, but I knew immediately he had won. There wouldn't be any victory for me this day.

Deacon had run the smarter race and would win the prize. Only two-tenths of a second separated us at the wire -- so, so close, but too far away to win. I was angry with myself; I must learn to make the right move at the right time. Mistakes couldn't be made at this level of competition, and the sooner I learned this the more races I would win. I had taken the last barrier awkwardly and that was why I had been beaten. Being angry makes men do foolish things, and I was no exception.

As soon as I recovered from the race, I moved to where they had placed one of the steeplechase barriers and started hurdling over it. Over and over again I jumped, becoming more and more tired but determined to punish myself. Finally, as I went into the hurdle, the inevitable happened: my calf muscle gave way and pain shot through my leg. I had torn something. The anger I had felt turned to frustration and I learned another bitter lesson the hard way. I was now paying its price.

Later I learned that my time of 8:47.8 was the fourth fastest ever by an American. It was little consolation now that I had injured myself. Furthermore, I realized that with the torn muscle, the rest of the summer could become a tragedy.

My leg was still sore when we reached Poland two days later. I was supposed to run the 5000-meter with Jim Beatty, who was scheduled to run the 1500 the first day and the 5000 the second. Other injuries and illness had reduced the number of athletes able to run, and every able-bodied man was pressed into service some like Jim into double duty.

On the first day, the 1500-meter was a classic. Jim was the favorite, but the Polish runners had other plans. At the outset the young Baran took the lead with the other Polish runner, Zimni, in second. Beatty settled into third with the other American in fourth during the first lap. At the start of the second lap, Baran upped the tempo and there was daylight between him and Zimni.

Zimni made no move to go with him and Baran began pulling away. Beatty, realizing he mustn't allow Baran to get too long a lead, started to pass Zimni. Immediately Zimni picked up the pace and Beatty, being on the turn, dropped back into third. As soon as he did, Zimni slowed and Beatty started around him again. It was now evident what the game was to be. The Polish runners didn't think they could beat Beatty in a regular race, but thought he might become shaken in a tactical effort.

The cat-and-mouse game went on for the entire lap -- even to the extent that Zimni would move Beatty out to the third lane when he started around. By now Baran had 30 yards on the field and was still inching away.

Starting into the straight toward the gun lap, Beatty made his move. With all the acceleration within him, he jumped Zimni before the other knew what was happening. In a flash he was by Zimni and after Baran. The question was whether he could catch him.

With 300 yards to go, Baran was beginning to tire; 200 to go and Beatty was closing; now, only 140 yards to go. Beatty was giving it all he had. The drive that made him such a great runner was bringing him in fast. Baran looked around and Jim was only five yards behind. At that moment it was evident Beatty was going to win.

Beatty had the momentum and the psychological edge. He would win without trouble. The race was fascinating for me. So this was international competition! This was what it was all about. It was indeed a cat-and-mouse game. A game for the mind as well as the body. This understanding made racing even more exciting. Not now, but someday, I would be strong enough to engage in a true tactical race. The race would be played like a chess match, where one strategy could be offset by a better move. Strength and speed were important, for without them, you couldn't play at all, but races would be won or lost by whichever runner was the best tactician.

The following day we went to the track in freezing rain. The track was completely under water as a maintenance crew worked to keep ahead of the downpour. It wasn't going to be a fun day for racing. In the training room I had my leg taped, but the pain was still there as I started warming up. I knew I would be running only to pick up the fourth and last place.

I never questioned the coach's decision why I was running. I was so happy just to be in international competition that I would do anything. Just a few months ago, I was a nobody. It was a surprise to place third in the national championships, and I hadn't realized my times had brought me to the elite of the U. S. distance runners. To be here was a thrill, and I wouldn't have passed up any opportunity to compete, even running at only 70 percent of my maximum.

The entire race was torture. From the standpoint of the leg and from being so far behind the other runners, I felt very low. Beatty put on a good show, though, staying with his main adversary, Zimni, and out kicking him to the tape.

I was glad it was over as we boarded a plane the next morning for England and our fourth dual meet. Because of the time change, my race was scheduled in less than 36 hours. My leg was feeling better, but it was still painful. It helped to know the doctor diagnosed the injury as a strain rather than a tear.

I was to run in the three-mile against Gordon Pirie and Bruce Tulloh, two of the world's best three-milers, as well as Max Truex. Even Truex wasn't given much of a chance against them, and of course, I wasn't even mentioned.

At the gun the two British runners took off together at a fast tempo and immediately left me behind. When I tried to push off my back foot, pain shot through my calf. It wasn't any use. I'd have to be content with running flat footed. To keep the leg from hurting too much, I limped slightly, and if I didn't go fast, the pain was kept to a minimum. Truex stayed with the Brits, who were trading leads.

As the race continued I fell further and further behind, until by the two-mile point, I was almost 200 meters back. Although my body was tight, I wasn't excessively tired, but could go no faster. It was so frustrating. I was a spectator as I looked across the track to watch the tactics being used. Max was running one of the best races of his life.

With one lap to go, Truex started to drop off. He had made a game effort, but the British had proven they were superior as they finished almost simultaneously. Truex was some 30 yards back. I was over 220 yards behind the winners, as was pointed out in the papers the next day:

"Pirie and Tulloh had an easy time of it in the three-mile as they easily beat Truex and waited to congratulate him at the finish fine." Then it went on to say: "All three men waited patiently for the tall, lanky American, Schul, to finish the race." It was bad enough just being in the race, but it was humiliating to have the whole world know of my plight.

I didn't know what the years had in store for me, but one thing was certain. I hoped never again to be an "also ran." The next time I attempted international competition, I wanted to be ready for any challenge.

Four

The Move To Los Angeles

In September 1961, when I returned from my first European tour to my home away from home at Oxnard Air Force Base, I'd been in the Air Force for two and one-half years. I found, to my delight, that Igloi had moved to Los Angeles and was training his runners at the University of Southern California. It was 60 miles south of the base, with a driving time of an hour and ten minutes. It would be quite a trip to train under him, but I was determined to have the best, and that was Igloi.

I set up a schedule for myself that was grueling. If the Air Force had known, I would have been on "KP" duty for a year. On Friday after finishing work I'd leave for Los Angeles about 4 p.m. I'd stay in the city and train throughout the weekend under Igloi, including early Monday morning. I would then drive back to the base, arriving by 7:30 a.m. to begin my work day.

On Monday evening, I drove to LA, returning after the 5:30 a.m. workout Tuesday morning. Tuesday evening I would head back to LA again and work out Tuesday night and Wednesday morning, again arriving back at the base by 7:30 a.m. Both Thursday workouts and the Friday morning workout were in the Oxnard area.

I wasn't the only one who woke at 5:30 in the morning those days; there were three or four of us working out at the same time.

On Friday afternoon the schedule would start over again. It wasn't easy and at times I thought I'd never make it. When I was on extra duty with the Air Force, it was really tough, and during the winter I never worked out during the day. Morning and evening the stars shone brightly and the moon was my companion. It wasn't so bad when I was in Los Angeles because Igloi was always there giving me encouragement. But the days I worked out at a local high school were very lonely. About once a week the State Highway Patrol would stop after seeing my car and shine their lights on the track. They would call me over and ask what I was doing. It was hard to explain as I didn't want to say I was training for the Olympics when that wasn't quite the case. They would just shake their heads as they went back to their patrol car.

I'd awaken at 5:15 a.m., slip into my running gear, quietly leave the barracks, and drive to Oxnard High School about five miles away. There I'd climb the fence, do the workouts Igloi had given me and drive back to the base to shower and eat breakfast with the other troops.

Because the Air Force, is mostly an eight-hour job, I'd report to my post and put in the eight-hour electronic job for which I had been trained. Immediately after work I'd again dress and drive to the track, arriving between 5 and 5:30 p.m. in the winter darkness. I would again spend one and a half to two hours doing the workout. All through the fall of that year and into 1962, the schedule remained the same.

That winter was the first time I would get an invitation to the big indoor meets, where I would be running against the world's top competition. The U. S. athletes, other than Beatty, weren't running the distance races well as yet. Consequently, when a foreigner such as New Zealand's Murray Halberg came to the U. S. he had little competition. My first race in the LA Invitational on Jan. 20 put me against Halberg and a schoolboy from Canada, Bruce Kidd, whom I would race many times.

As expected, Halberg won easily. I was second in 8:53.3. Later that year Kidd beat me in a close race at the *Chicago Daily News* relays, with my now close friend, Laszlo Tabori, placing third. The next night in Milwaukee I won the two-mile against Tabori in 8:58.2. With that race, my indoor season came to a close because the meet directors wouldn't accept any more of my entries. They wouldn't take a chance with a newcomer.

The outdoor season started in April, and I kept up my strenuous schedule so I could continue training with Igloi. It was a Spartan existence. I did little else but work, eat, sleep, and train. There was no time to date or to have any kind of a social life, because I was always too tired. My commanders were always asking me why I was so thin and didn't seem to have much energy. Of course, I couldn't tell them why because it was against regulations for me to travel more than 30 miles from the base at any time, and I was going 60 miles, three times a week.

The first big race of the outdoor season in Southern California is the Mt. San Antonio College relays. I was looking forward to the competition and Igloi thought I was in very good condition. I would run the 3000-meter steeplechase.

"Bob, we are to try for American record in this race." he stated.

I looked at him with some disbelief, but I trusted him so much that if he said I was ready, there was no question I could do it.

"The American record?" I asked.

"Yes, there is but no question in my mind you are ready. You have progressed very fast. You are ready." was his reply.

That week prior to the meet wasn't easy. Igloi didn't let us rest except for the very major competitions, but I was feeling good and possessed a newly found confidence. I knew now that I had arrived on the American scene in distance running and had moved up considerably in the "pecking order" of what was now the Los Angeles Track Club.

On the day of the race, because it was only a little more than an hour from LA to Mt. San Antonio Junior College, several of us piled into a car and made our way through the heavy traffic on to the San Bernardino Freeway east to Pomona.

When we arrived some of the preliminaries had already begun, so we relaxed in what little stadium shade there was. The finals were to start in the early afternoon, but that wasn't a problem because it was late April and the sun wasn't overly hot. A few hours later came warm-up time, and I headed for the west end of the track where there was a large area of grass. I felt good as I warmed up an hour before the race. I moved slowly, allowing my body muscles to become loose and warm Then, with 15 minutes to go, I did a few medium sprints and settled down to await the call to the starting line.

There were almost a dozen athletes in the race. My teammate Dave Martin and I wore the colors of the Los Angeles Track Club. Dave had been a teammate of mine several years earlier when I was a freshman at Miami University in Oxford, Ohio and had since graduated from the University of Michigan. He had decided that if he was ever going to improve he must have good coaching, so he had come to LA to take a job and to train with Igloi.

At the start of the race, I immediately took the lead as Igloi had authorized. It was a good, comfortable pace, and with each lap, I was placing distance between myself and the others. With three laps to go I was 50 yards in front of Dave, and he had broken away from the others. I also knew I was running fast enough to break the American record. Then it happened.

One minute I was feeling very strong and the next, I felt like my body had just been drained of all its energy. I wasn't hurting; there wasn't the pain of fatigue. I felt more like a clock that was running down, going slower and slower until the spring had no tension. I struggled on, trying to increase my tempo, but it was no use. Dave was closing on me, and finally, with 150 yards to go near the last water jump, he passed me. He beat me by five yards. I wondered about myself. Was Igloi wrong? Maybe I wasn't in the condition he thought. I cooled down, feeling exhausted.

For the next two weeks the workouts were very tiring, but I assumed my body wasn't recovering from the strenuous training. Then at the end of a Thursday workout, Igloi called Beatty, Jim Grelle, and me over to him.

"This Saturday we will run in Southern Pacific AAU; you know this," he stated. "We going to break world record for the two-mile."

I stood there listening, for I now understood that these statements weren't just idle talk. When Igloi said we were ready, we were ready and I dismissed my race at Mt. SAC as a fluke.

"Jim Beatty, he is ready now," he continued, "and you, you two will help break this mark."

He pointed at Jim Grelle and me. That was all. By turning away he dismissed us. Nothing else was said about it until race time.

On Saturday evening we arrived at Occidental College for the race. Only 3,500 spectators were in the stadium as it was essentially a local meet. After we warmed up for our customary hour, we went to Igloi's side. There were only two minutes to go. We took off our sweats and checked our spikes to see if they were tied properly. We stood there awaiting our orders. I wasn't too concerned as we listened.

"Grelle, you will lead first mile in four minutes, 15 seconds. Beatty, you will take fifth lap, and, Bob, you will take sixth lap to give Jim rest. After you do this, you are on your own." He looked directly into my eyes. "Bob, you must maintain tempo."

I felt very excited by Igloi's speech. I could feel the adrenaline flow now, but I must control it. It mustn't be wasted. We stepped onto the track and the starter lined us up. Igloi's runners comprised half the field of 12.

Grelle jumped into the lead with Beatty on his heels. I was third, and into the second lap I was having a hard time staying with them. We went through four laps with Grelle only missing his assignment by .01 of a second. Now it was Beatty's turn, but then I could see Igloi shouting that I should take the lead now. He must have seen what I felt, for I was tearing myself apart and losing energy fast.

I swung away from Beatty's heels and with all that was in me, took the lead. There was no use fooling myself, I was finished. I wanted to hold on so badly. I forced myself around the turn and into the back stretch. I was running the lap as if it were my last. I could feel Beatty on my shoulder, coaxing me to go faster. I was all out. This was it and I couldn't do it.

Around the turn and into the front side we came and immediately I moved to the second lane. Beatty, and then Grelle, easily moved by me. I almost collapsed as they moved away. I watched them as they put yards between us, moving effortlessly. I struggled on, watching them. Three more laps to go, and once again, I was just a spectator, as was the fourth man, yards behind.

Beatty set a new world record in 8:29.8. Grelle ran a fine race to finish second in 8:36; I was third in just under nine minutes. I couldn't figure out what was wrong. Was it that I wasn't in shape to cover the first part of a race that fast? I thought I should have been closer, but after talking with Igloi, he just shook his head as he said, "Bob, you in great shape, I do not understand."

My next competition was in the Air Force championships in Texas in two weeks. We left California in an Air Force C-130 and traveled to Sheppard Air Force Base a few days before the meet. I was feeling weak, but thought it would pass. I'd see a doctor when I arrived in Texas.

Being an enlisted man, I joined the other noncommissioned officers in shabby barracks, while the officers on the team had the air-conditioned officer's quarters, a very unfair and discriminatory practice. By this time, I was sicker, and the next day I made an appointment to see the base medical officer.

After checking me over, he prescribed an antibiotic and sent me on my way. I was told I might be a little weak for the competition, but I would be fine. My throat was so sore, I couldn't swallow my saliva; the only thing that would go down was ice cream.

A day later the competition began in the evening hours. It was the only time the meet could be run because the daytime temperature was over 100 degrees. All day long I lay on my bed taking aspirin every couple of hours.

An hour before I was to run my first race, the mile, I took three more aspirin and went to warm up. I could hardly move I was so weak, spending most of the time trying to loosen up my legs. Fortunately competition was lacking, and I fell in behind the leader for most of the race. I gave it everything I had to win in the last 60 yards. I won in 4:30, quite a comedown, for Igloi thought I was in shape to run close to 4 minutes.

Afterward I headed for the barracks to rest and to wait until the next evening when I was to run the 880. I didn't sleep much that night as I tossed and turned in the extreme heat. The next day I again bought a pint of ice cream and continued taking aspirin. I still couldn't eat solid food and my throat hadn't improved at all. That evening the routine leading up to the race was the same as before, aspirin and some easy jogging to loosen up.

The race tactics were also the same as I stayed behind until the last straight away, then out-kicked the field. I won again in 1:59, a time I had done in workouts when running 880 repeats.

Whatever was wrong had to change for the better because the

national championship meet was a week away at Mt. San Antonio College in California. By virtue of winning these races, I automatically qualified for that meet. The next day we flew the C-130 to Pomona College, where we'd be staying. I was sick the entire way, lying under the seats of the aircraft, not caring if someone opened the door and threw me out. I thought the flight would never end, and I was never so happy to land after that plane trip.

When we arrived, I immediately went to see the doctor on duty. After that visit, I knew my racing was over for the year. I was so very disheartened when I told Max Dr. Dooley didn't know exactly what was wrong but strongly advised against running and to see the base physician as soon as possible. Max told me to call a friend of his, Dr. Harry Silver, who was a doctor for the Southern California Striders. I did, just as soon as I returned to my apartment in LA.

I told Dr. Silver my symptoms: "I don't have any energy during my races and I'm tired all the time. My throat is so sore I can't even swallow."

We talked a while longer and then he gave me the bad news, suggesting the strong possibility of mononucleosis. He wanted a blood test to be sure.

"Copy this number down and call the lab," he said. "Tell them to set an appointment up as soon as possible and that you're my patient."

When I told him I didn't have any money to pay for the lab test, he told me not to worry about the expense. He said he'd call the lab and I was to call them in five minutes. Later I discovered that Dr. Silver had paid for my test.

Here was a man I had never met, but he cared enough to do what he thought best for me. Some day I wanted to meet this man and thank him personally.

After the test, I drove back to the apartment feeling despondent. They wouldn't have the results until the following morning and they'd let Dr. Silver know as soon as possible. Once again I slept fitfully and the next morning I waited for what seemed an eternity. That afternoon the phone rang.

"Bob, this is Dr. Silver and I've got the results of your test."

I listened, breathlessly awaiting the outcome that would determine my immediate future.

"I'm afraid I have some bad news for you. Your tests show that you do have mono, and the lab said it was one of the worse cases they've ever seen. I suggest that you return immediately to the Air Force base and report your condition to the medical officer there."

I listened without really hearing.

"Bob, do you understand what I'm saying?"

"I'm sorry, Doctor, yes, I understand."

I was fighting back tears as I hung up the phone. I'd not only missed the national championships where I was supposed to place in the top two to make the U. S. team, but Igloi had put together a trip to Europe for his top runners. Six of us were to go, and now I would have to miss that, too. The trip was even more important to me than meeting the Soviet team at Palo Alto in a couple of weeks.

Everything was finished, and I had thoughts of giving up running forever; I was in such despair. Since my last race, I had three days rest and was feeling much better, but Dr. Silver told me not to take that as an indication that all was well. Reluctantly I had to see Igloi before I left for Oxnard. I had taken the blood test on Friday and it was now Saturday afternoon. The nationals had been held Friday and Saturday so I decided to stay overnight and see Igloi at the track Sunday morning during regular training.

That evening my roommates returned to the apartment with the news of the championships, and I listened dejectedly as they told me that George Young had taken first. The second place person, I had beaten all season. That made me feel even worse.

The next morning I went to see Igloi. He was not into a hard workout as many of the athletes had competed over the weekend. I approached him, and when he saw me, he came to meet me.

"Well, what did doctor say?"

"Bad news, Coach." I answered. "I have to report to the base hospital because I have what is called mononucleosis." Several other athletes had gathered around by that time and listened as I spoke.

Igloi was as disappointed as I. He now understood why my races had gone downhill all spring. As we talked he told me that Dave Martin would take my place on the squad for Europe.

As I walked along the field I was in emotional misery. Ever since Igloi had announced the trip to Europe, I had been ecstatic.

Not only would it have been a fun trip, but I would have learned so much. I felt I'd been given a great present, only to have it snatched away. As Dave approached to ask what the doctor had said, I told him the coach wanted to see him.

Dave went to Igloi and was told he'd be taking my place on the trip to Europe. I watched him as he started to jog again after the news. His step seemed lighter and he was a happy man. He sincerely expressed his regrets to me, and being a good friend, I was glad he was next in line to go. Dave went to the far side of the track to continue his workout. In the next few moments, though, the most bizarre thing happened.

He was doing 100-yard repeats along the far side of the football field as Rink Babka threw a discus in his direction. Dave didn't know what hit him as the discus took one bounce and chopped into his legs. Dave went down as if a bullet had slammed into him and his scream filled the air. We all ran to him and fell silent when we saw the bottom part of his leg lying at an angle. It was broken.

Someone ran to get a car. Dave had gone into shock as he sat holding his leg. The car was driven as close to Dave as possible, and very gently we loaded him into it to get him to the hospital as quickly as possible.

It was indeed so bizarre that within minutes Igloi had lost two of his best runners. I would return at a future date, but Dave would never run another race. It was difficult to understand the mystery of this tragedy.

That evening the other men and I discussed Dave's horrible accident and my own untimely illness. We agreed that there were certainly many worse things happening in the world, but this was happening to us. Trying to put these events into proper perspective was difficult for me as I had looked at the trip as one of the greatest highlights of my life. I'm sure Dave had felt the same, even if only for a few brief moments.

The next morning I reported to the base dispensary at Oxnard and was given another blood test. I was immediately placed in bed. I read about the championships in the papers and a week later watched on television as the U. S. team, the team I should have been on, met the Russians at Stanford. Instead, I was in quarantine and as I watched the contest, tears filled my eyes. I thought about what could have been and it made me more determined than ever to get back into training.

No matter how bad it was, I must never give up but instead think of the future. However, that wasn't to be for a long while because I was to stay in the infirmary from mid-June through mid-August. Each week they tested my blood and told me it wasn't yet back to normal. It was so boring after I had been used to pushing my body under Igloi's training. I would stare at the ceiling for hours just as I had done when I'd first begun Igloi's method, but this time I was waiting for my body to heal.

FIVE

Starting Over

Doctors told me to take it easy for a month, with no physical activity, when I was released from the infirmary the middle of August. For someone like me that was very difficult to do. With all that rest I felt mentally good and eager to get back into training. I didn't dwell on all the past training that seemingly had gone to waste, but focused on the positive, contemplating how to begin.

The next evening, I walked to the back of the base where there once was an old track. The entire area was covered with sage brush but paths remained. This would be the place to regain my physical strength. Even though I felt weak, my brain was in command.

I had trouble jogging for more than 20 minutes. When I finished I was totally exhausted. I knew I couldn't give in to this fatigue so I gradually pushed myself to do more. Within two weeks I felt much better and was up to 50 minutes at a faster pace. By mid-September I felt strong enough to begin serious training. Igloi, who had just returned from Europe, agreed to begin training together again.

He took it easy on me for the first week as he evaluated my condition. After that he really poured it on, taking no pity on me. It was like the first time I had met him but now I knew what to expect. This time I was prepared to take anything he gave me. I took a lot of kidding that first week, for I had gained weight in the posterior part of my body. I guess the guys wanted to help me lose this "loose rump," and I was black and blue after a few days as Beatty, Grelle and the others took potshots at me as they went by. The kidding made the work easier and within a few weeks, I had returned to my running weight.

Most of the time we were in serious training. Igloi would have it no other way. At the same time, we could always kid one another and smile when fatigue was heavy on the body. Those were hard days but often also full of the mysteries of what we could accomplish, days we could only live once and dreams that could never be brought back. What kept us going was the close association with each other. It is easier to suffer when you see others suffering. It is hard to falter when others aren't. We lived those days together on the training field, finding solace in each other, literally training to beat the world.

As September moved into October and then into November, the days became shorter and the workouts longer as Igloi pushed us unmercifully. We hated and loved it at the same time. We hated it because it was grueling, but loved it because we were in command of our powerful machines -- our bodies! Most of us never saw the sun anymore because our jobs made us train in the early morning and late in the evening. It was a hard life, but we had Igloi and each other

The doctors had told me a person can only contact mono one time if completely cured. But the driving of 120 miles three times weekly had taken its toll, and I decided not to travel as much as before. Igloi would give me workouts scribbled on a scrap of paper, and I'd follow them to the letter. I came to LA on Tuesday and Friday nights only now, sleeping on the floor of an apartment rented by a college friend of mine, Nick Kitt, who was also training under Igloi.

As my conditioning improved, I decided if I were to run a good indoor season, I'd have train under Igloi full time. Therefore, I applied for a month's leave of absence for December, days that I had accumulated, and worked at a large department store during the day to earn extra money -- my Air Force salary was only $78.00 a month.

That December was as hard as any month I can remember working under Igloi. He wanted me ready for the indoor season, too. I wasn't a superstar, however, and certainly was not in the same class as Beatty and Grelle, so I wouldn't be invited to all the top meets around the country.

My first race in January 1963 came at the Los Angeles Invitational. Although we didn't have the best team, I anchored the two-mile relay for the LA Track Club in 1:53. My other run in February, the two-mile, went well and I easily won in 8:51.6.

The next weekend was the big one for me, the national AAU championships to be held in Madison Square Garden in New York City. Igloi thought I was in good shape, and I felt as though I could run a good race. My mental attitude was right. The big names were Kidd from Canada, who later scratched, Max Truex, Michel Bernard of France, Peter McArdle, a resident of New York, and Pat Clohessy from Australia. I still felt I had a chance of winning the three-mile.

The first mile went in 4:32, with the lead changing every lap. The second mile slowed considerably as we went through in 9:16.2. With two and one half laps to go, about 400 yards, the Frenchman picked up the pace and sprinted to the lead. Clohessy couldn't go with him. Before I could move out and around Clohessy, Bernard had 10 yards on me and was pulling away. At first I couldn't gain a step, but with only a little over 60 yards to go, I started catching the Frenchman.

As we came around the final curve, I was gaining fast but there just wasn't enough track left; Bernard held me off by a few feet. He ran 13:38.4 and I was happy with my time, posting a personal best of 13:38.8. I wasn't happy with my race, however, because I had made a mistake in tactics. I should have won; Bernard had run the smarter race and I had to be content with second. Since Bernard was a foreigner, I became the U. S. champion but that was little consolation.

On March 8, the club traveled to Chicago where Beatty was to try for the two-mile world record. I was also to run, but Igloi had told me to stay off the pace for he knew Beatty was unbeatable.

Beatty took off with the rest of us strung out behind. It was a good field, with Witold Baran of Poland and Bruce Kidd in the race. Both tried to stay with Beatty. It was no contest after the first lap as Beatty pulled away. At three-quarters of a mile, Kidd and

Baran were 10 yards back, while I was another 10 yards behind them.

Beatty had run 4:13.5 for the mile and I had been just over 4:22. I felt sluggish during the first mile, but now I felt better. The crowd of over 13,000 cheering for Beatty also gave me a lift. At one and one half miles I closed on Kidd and Baran and was ready to challenge for second. As I moved in on them, Baran stepped off the track, calling it a night. I moved past Kidd and could see Beatty running effortlessly 60 yards in front. Something else was happening: I was beginning to close the gap.

This meant nothing to anyone in the field house, except me, as all eyes were on Beatty and the clock. But it gave me more confidence and I was encouraged as I continued to drive harder. I knew I couldn't catch Beatty; he set a world record of 8:30.7, but I posted the third fastest time ever run of 8:37.5 with a second mile of 4:15.5. I was elated when I learned the time, and as Beatty was taking his victory lap, Igloi was the first to congratulate me, "Fantastic!" He was as happy with my performance as he was with Beatty's. Well, maybe almost.

We celebrated with lots of talk and laughter over dinner that even-ing. Igloi had a new world record for one of his runners and not a bad time for his second one. Oh, this was fun! The hard work was paying off. I had called home before we left for dinner and talked to Mom as she kept relaying the news to Dad. I could hear Dad in the background and could tell they were really proud of my accomplishments.

As I returned to Los Angeles from Chicago to continue my training, I found that my left calf was sore. Not again, I thought. Because of my performances in Chicago and the national championships, I had been chosen to be on the U. S. team for the Pan American Games to be held in Sao Paulo, Brazil. I hoped this injury wouldn't keep me home again.

Trying to continue my training, I knew workouts had to be changed. All speed work was eliminated and the entire work load was shortened. Igloi deliberated over my condition and wondered if I shouldn't pass up the trip because I wouldn't be in the best running shape. Beatty and Grelle came to my assistance and argued that even injured I was still in better shape than any other American who could take my place. Igloi finally gave in and agreed I should go. YES!

After congregating in the beautiful vacation spot of Miami Beach, Coach Igloi and the rest of the athletes arrived in the South American city of Sao Paulo. We were to stay in a new complex being built by the government as part of a new university. We were very excited about residing in their new facility, but not prepared for what awaited us.

When we arrived we found the building was not completed. The shell of it was up but there was no glass in the windows. We could hardly believe it. This was to be our home for the next two weeks? Although very disappointed we had no choice but to stay. We had 12 athletes in a two-room arrangement separated by a thin wall.

As in all cases when this happens on a trip, the distance runners try to stay together because of our demanding schedule. This requires us to go to bed earlier than the other athletes. Six of us, therefore, were crowded into one side of the room, with little space to walk. It wasn't going to be the most pleasant of trips, but we would make the most of it. We didn't know we were in for still more surprises.

A few of the weight men moved into the other half of the room and found that their shower didn't work. When we tested ours, we found only a trickle of water coming out of the pipe. Then there was the dangerous situation of the hot water being heated by an electrical heater at the nozzle; we could have been electrocuted.

With no glass in the windows, that night we were invaded by what seemed to be a million mosquitoes. We slept miserably, with the mosquitoes buzzing around our heads. Buried under covers, it was miserably hot. But every time you stuck your head out they were waiting.

When we awoke crumpled and bedraggled, we asked our team manager if he could find something to help us out. He remembered the Olympic committee had sent along a few boxes of mosquito repellent. It was really funny when we opened the box; there was enough to last us for five years. Someone on the Olympic Committee must have been to South America before.

Well, the stuff really solved the problem, for every night we saturated ourselves in it. We really stank and with all of us in that small room together; it was repulsive. But no mosquito, or anything else for that matter, came within two blocks of us after that.

Every morning and evening Igloi's athletes along with a few others arranged transportation to an athletic club in downtown Sao Paulo for training. It was a beautiful place with a huge clubhouse, a track, two swimming pools with diving towers and three-meter boards, various tennis courts, soccer fields and anything else the membership needed.

Facilities such as this are very much needed in various parts of the United States. We could then produce even greater athletes, sending teams of all sports into international competition on a par with any country in the world. I thought how the LA Track Club had to almost beg to train on university or high school facilities and then be rudely treated. Having to become expert at climbing fences and dodging water sprinklers only served to frustrate the athletes and many quit in disgust.

Even though the facilities in Sao Paulo were great, I had arrived with my calf muscle still sore, and our medical staff couldn't help me. The specialized equipment for treatment of injuries had been left in Miami and wouldn't arrive until a week later, too late to help me or anyone else.

As the contest began the next week, everyone knew which country would have the most medals -- the United States. Because of our size, we always dominated the games. The other countries rarely showed any power. Track and field was a U. S. show, and Grelle and Beatty led a one-two sweep of the 1500 meter race.

Now it was time for the 5000 meter race. I had the trainer tape my leg as he had done for every workout that week. It seemed my leg had become worse, but as long as the race wasn't too fast, I thought it would hold together.

It was a slow pace with no one wanting the lead. After the first 200 yards, I took over, but realized I wasn't going to be able to push hard. The first mile was slow as we came through in 4:40. Nobody would become tired at this rate and I wanted to pick up the pace but every time I attempted it, I'd get shooting pains in my calf. The second mile continued in the same slow fashion.

Finally, with three laps to go, Charlie Clark of the United States took the lead. He picked up the tempo slightly, but then slowed again. With two laps left, I regained the lead and tried once more to up the tempo, but I could only get a little more speed out of the leg. When I tried to drive off my toes, the pain would start.

There were 300 yards to go now and I was closely followed by Clark and Suarez of Argentina. As we headed into the final turn, Suarez started sprinting and Clark followed. All I could do was watch them go. As I crossed the finish line, I wasn't breathing hard at all, but my body was tight from not being able to relax. I had won the bronze medal, but it held no glory for me. I was frustrated because I should have won the gold. Again, injury was my downfall.

The games were almost over, but in the final days the competition between the United States and the Cuban baseball team extended beyond the field of play. Coming back on the same bus after a very close contest, two of the players exchanged blows, and the entire bus erupted. It was the last time the teams rode together. We were extremely glad to be returning to the United States.

Back in LA I tried to continue my training, but all I could do was easy jogging. I began to lose the endurance I had built up over the fall and winter. The national AAU meet was fast approaching in St. Louis, and I wanted to be ready for the 5000. Week after week went by with the leg slowly improving. I worried that it would not heal in time. As the deadline for the entries approached, I had a long conversation with Igloi. There was no getting around it; my leg wasn't healed enough and if I were to race, I would risk further injury. For the second year in a row, I was to miss the national championships. These were the times when I resolved not to be mentally defeated, but it was difficult.

Again, I had a 99 percent chance of making the U. S. team, the second best two and three-miler behind Beatty, who was going to run the mile. Going home that night, I gave serious thought to quitting, for it seemed that when all the important races came around I was either sick or injured. What was the use of training so hard and then missing all the fun? After some soul searching, I knew I'd really never give up. I couldn't give in. I knew I was competitive and I wanted to prove I could be one of the best.

The AAU meet was over and the team selected, and as I looked at the winner's time in the three-mile, it was assured that I would have made the team. The winning time was 13:45.4, and I had run much faster in the indoor three-mile the previous February.

As the athletes toured Europe that summer, I was trying to get my leg back into shape. Slowly it came around until all the pain had vanished. Now it was back to the hard grind, picking up where we had left off before the Pan American Games. I was very eager to get back into competition and felt really good.

On Aug. 1, Igloi put me into a two-mile with several other LA Track Club athletes. A good race, I won in 8:46.6. Two weeks later in another all-comers meet, I ran 8:44.6, which was to be the fastest American time that year.

Now I came to a crossroad and had a big decision to make. I'd been out of the Air Force for nine months now and had been working as a salesman for Colgate Palmolive Co. in their soap division. It wasn't the type of work I wanted for the rest of my life, and I wasn't a very good salesman anyway. Also, the day I left the Air Force, when I least expected it, love had entered my life.

The first time I saw Sharon she was walking towards our apartment building with her roommate. I figured they were new tenants who had just moved in.

My friend and roommate Joe Douglas and I had just returned from the store carrying groceries when I saw her. She was about 5 feet 2, had dark hair, was small boned and was very cute. I told Joe, "You can have the one on the left, but leave the one on the right alone." It took some time before I had a chance to talk to her but we finally met in the courtyard. We liked each other right away.

I discovered she had grown up in Boise, Idaho and had come to LA several years ago to make a better life for herself. She was a secretary for a company in downtown LA. We talked at every opportunity and eventually I asked her out on a date. We went to the movies and took walks and started eating meals together. I found it easy to talk with Sharon and I told her all about my racing. She said she really enjoyed hearing about it. Sharon was caring, sweet, and fairly quiet. We enjoyed many months in each other's company; double dating with Jim Grelle and his wife.

Eventually everything came together and we decided to get married.

We asked the Grelles to stand up for us and Jim Beatty and Joe

Douglas were two of the ushers. Only our mothers would be able to fly in for our wedding. When Sharon met Mom before the wedding, they took to each other right away. On the other hand, it took Sharon's mother some time before getting used to me. It would be over a year before either of us would meet each other's fathers.

It was a memorable occasion not only for us but for Igloi as well. This was to be the first time he would see his wife and children since he had left Hungary in 1956. For seven long years, he had tried to get their release from the Hungarian government; finally his family had received permission to emigrate.

They arrived at the Los Angeles airport just in time to be driven to the church for our wedding reception. It was, indeed, heartwarming to see Coach Igloi as happy as I was that day.

In August I had to make the decision whether to remain in California or to go back to Miami University in Oxford, Ohio, to finish my education. It was a hard decision to make, for Igloi had been like a father to me. He had taught me how to mentally push myself when I was tired and had been the one to offer the most encouragement when I was sick or injured. He never failed to tell us he saw in us the potential to become great runners.

Also, it was a time of transition, for the club was losing some of its top runners. Truex had retired to study law, Tabori was forced to retire because of bad legs, Beatty moved back to North Carolina to seek political office and Grelle was talking about moving back to Portland, Ore., his boyhood home. Although there were still many athletes training under Igloi, the group that had done so many things together was gone.

When I walked on the training field that late August day to tell Igloi my decision, I felt miserable. Here was the man who was responsible for making me what I was as a runner and I was going to tell him I was leaving. It had to be done, for I couldn't allow my education to suffer, but it was one of the toughest moments of my life. Igloi was a coach among coaches. I've been around many coaches during my running career, but none came close to having the knowledge he possessed or the dedication that made athletics his life.

He was on the track at 5 a.m., training athletes who had early starting times at their jobs. He would again be on the field at 4:30

p.m. I never saw him late for our 5 p.m. workout. He would stay until the last runner had finished his workout, usually around 7:30 p.m. Once a 33-year-old runner couldn't work out until 7 p.m. because of his job. They would both be there in the darkness, just the two of them, with Igloi giving training orders to a runner who had seen better days. He was that kind of a man.

In between workouts Igloi was kept busy putting training schedules into individual workout books he kept on all the runners. From time to time during discussions at his home he would bring out the books and show us his predictions for our futures. He was tough and he didn't like his boys to play around when training; but all who could take the vigorous schedule respected him and would do anything he asked.

In the fall of 1962, Igloi started having pain which was diagnosed as a double inguinal hernia. I suppose it had been with him for many years, but now it had become acute. All of us were constantly urging him to have corrective surgery. A doctor in the area was going to perform the surgery free, but Igloi refused, stating it was important he be with us in our training.

This went on month after month until he had trouble standing, even for short periods. Often we could see the pain etched on his face as we ran by. He never liked to sit while we were running. He thought it was his duty to be on his feet; only if he were in absolute agony would he finally find some relief by sitting in the stands.

When the doctor finally convinced him to have the operation since gangrene was now a possibility, he still waited until the cross-country season was over. A little more than a week later he was back at the track, sitting in his car, watching and giving instructions to his athletes. He was truly a loving, dedicated, and caring person and because of the tremendous respect I held for him, both as a coach and as a man, my heart was very heavy as I bid him goodbye.

SIX

Back In Ohio

On Sept. 1 Sharon and I left Los Angeles and returned to Oxford, Ohio and Miami University. My wife was very understanding and quite sympathetic at my leaving Los Angeles and Igloi, and we talked about our future during the 2,500-mile drive home.

Since I was married, I was more serious about life, which meant I would be spending more time on my studies. I was more serious about my running, also, and I'd be spending more time in training than before. Marriage didn't change that, of course.

Fortunately, I was still eligible for competition in the spring and the University agreed to lend me books and to pay for my tuition. But there was a big concern. I was by far the best collegiate distance runner in the United States and was afraid I wouldn't face the competition I needed to improve. That was a big problem in the U. S. as there were so few good people in the distances. That fact alone held us back. I hadn't been able to compete against the best Europeans and I was concerned that without this competition I might not improve as quickly.

In the meantime, we also had to work out our financial concerns and tried to devise a strategy that would meet all our needs. Sharon and I had saved a small amount of money which would go for our apartment and food until she could find a job on campus. She was hired as a secretary at the placement center for graduating seniors at

$200 a month, working 40 hours a week. It was quite a come-down for her as she had been making $550 a month in Los Angeles as a private secretary. We were lucky, though, for her to get work, because the job market was scarce in this small college town.

Arrangements had been made through the athletic department to reserve one of the housing units for married couples. It was a one-room combination of living room, bedroom, dining room, and cooking area in a 14 x 22-foot space. The bath was enclosed in one corner of the room. The Hotel Hilton it was not, but we were young and tolerant and it was inexpensive.

The next morning I went out for my daily training and afterward went to the athletic department to meet the new track and field head coach, Bob Epscamp, who had replaced the retired George Rider a couple of years earlier.

Upon returning to Miami I had planned to train myself following the Igloi system, but for the first week I joined the Miami cross-country team for their daily workouts. Only a few of them did twice-a-day workouts and even they would miss quite often. Bob Epscamp was providing workouts for my training but he started missing the ones at 6 a.m. I was training myself more and more frequently until finally I decided to tell Bob I thought it best to train myself. That was fine with him and since my workouts were quite different from the team's, I decided to use an area removed from their training site.

I found such a place near our apartment. It was the ladies' field hockey area. There were three fields in a line and the distance from one end to the other was about 330 yards. I decided to do all my running on the straight and after a few months found it curtailed injuries.

Like Igloi, I used 100, 150, 220, and 330 distances most of the time. When I wanted to run a 440, I'd go to the track or just make a swing around the fields. The track gave me the opportunity to get away from the same old area. Under this system I was only on the track about once every two weeks, usually on a Sunday morning. I'd drag Sharon with me and give her a stopwatch. She would sleepily look at the watch, yawning, but was very good-natured about it. She was a great source of encouragement to me.

These became my test days and it was the only time I was under the watch. On most of those occasions, I'd test myself for conditioning by doing repeat 440s. Soon I was able to do 20 quarters (with 160-yard intervals) averaging between 60-61 seconds for the first 19 repeats and then sprinting the last one all out. I was always between 54 and 55 seconds for the last 440.

Many times I'd be able to finish all 20 without a great amount of fatigue. By treating it as a test I could determine whether my body conditioning was improving. I was still on the Igloi schedule of training twice a day, Monday through Saturday, with only one workout on Sunday. Since I had an 8 a.m. class I was training at 6 a.m. As the fall continued the average times became a little faster and my intervals a little shorter. It was a beautiful, crisp fall that year, and I used every day of it to good advantage.

I began thinking about the Olympics and was wondering if this was to be my year. I hoped so as I began workouts I had never attempted under Igloi. He had laid the foundation and now it was up to me to finish the job. I was determined to make him proud of his pupil.

As the first week of December came around, the first real snows started to fall. My days of running on the fields would soon be over, and I'd have to find another place to train. We didn't have an indoor arena and I wasn't going to run on the roads as I'd done as a freshman and sophomore. I realized my legs and feet were too fragile for that type of pounding and I'd have to find a softer surface.

Luckily, I found two. The first was the oldest building on campus, built in the 1800s as a ladies' gym. It was now used by the ROTC. At the top of the small gymnasium was a running track, unused for many years. It was about four feet wide and 100 yards in circumference; the turns weren't even banked. To take the turns, it would be necessary to slow to a jog. My first thought was never to use this track but I changed my mind quickly when the temperatures dropped below zero.

The second place I found to run was under the stands at the football stadium. Although there wasn't much room there, I'd run there several years earlier and found I could put it to good use. The area that could be used for training was about 65 yards in length with a brick wall at one end and a shot-put ring at the other. It was approximately 12 yards wide with steel posts positioned down the center that supported the stands. The only problem was the dirt floor was heavy with dust. Bob Epscamp agreed he'd have oil poured on it which would also help keep it softer. I thought of that beautiful sports facility in Sao Paulo and sighed.

I used this dirt surface after the snows came. Eventually the cold winter air forced me to take refuge indoors during the morning training. What a job it was to change into my running clothes: two pairs of sweat pants and two sweat shirts, one with a hood that I wore over a stocking cap. Sharon had sewn a unique face guard over one of the hoods with some red flannel that wouldn't irritate my face. The first morning, however, I ran into problems as I sucked the cloth into my mouth each time I inhaled.

Using a little imagination, I found some light copper wire and ran it in and out throughout the fabric. Now I could fashion the material into any shape I wanted and it worked perfectly. As I exhaled, the warm air would be trapped in a small pocket I had formed and would re-warm the air I was breathing into my lungs. As an asthmatic, cold air always caused me problems. I'd begin wheezing soon after any exertion. Now I wouldn't have to worry about it.

Over my hands I wore wool socks that seemed to be the best insulator and the most comfortable to wear. I received some funny looks. I looked like a creature from outer space, especially the mouth part of the face guard.

The Ohio weather during that part of the year can be intense and that winter was rough. The worst part was waking up at 6 a.m., stumbling around in the dark, getting ready for the session and then opening the front door of our apartment. The icy wind hit me without mercy. The stars were still bright as I stepped outside. Only the wind could be heard for no one else on campus was up at this hour. I drove our car to the training spot which was only a half mile away for I didn't want to spend extra time in the cold after my workout. I'd be sweating profusely and would become chilled very quickly. On those occasions when the weather was too bitter, I used the indoor track in the old gym.

At those inclement times, only the janitor was in the building. He would unlock the door to let me in and then go back to his duties. We both went to work for the next one and one half hours, he doing his job and I doing mine. Around and around I'd go, trying to keep my mind off the number of laps. I'd run for five minutes and jog for one, then run for ten and jog for two. It was the most boring routine I had ever done. I'd try to pick up speed on the straights not only to get rid of the boredom but to increase my heart rate as well.

Most afternoons I could train on the dirt area because the days would warm up enough to make it comfortable. As I arrived around 5 p.m. all the other runners had already finished their sessions and I was alone. This was best because there wasn't much room and I needed to get as much speed into the workout as possible.

To warm up I'd jog easy for 10 minutes and then do 10 times a straight away. The most I could get out of the straight was 50 yards, and I had to slow to make the turn. After that, I'd begin my sets. They were different from what I had done on the grass, but the theory was the same. I'd do such things as 16 laps, running "fresh" down one side and "good" up the other. Then I'd jog for five minutes and begin something else. I'd spend an hour and a half or more running in this small circle. It was definitely not all that pleasant.

December went well, however, and I was progressing in my conditioning. How long I could continue to progress under the weather conditions was debatable and I decided to use the indoor season to keep me sharp. That would mean entering as many races as I could.

Although the distance races would make the following months very tiring, which meant I might not run well in all races, I had to break the monotony of training. I therefore decided to write the necessary letters to the meet directors.

The first race wasn't to be indoors but the last outdoor meet of the year on December 28 in the Sugar Bowl Invitational. It was to be a 5000-meter race and the competition didn't appear to be too rough.

I arrived in New Orleans the day before the race feeling good in the warmer weather. My competition would come from USC's Julio Marin, who was the publicity favorite in the race; Bill Straub of the Air Force Academy; and Mel Robinson, who had been a teammate of mine under Igloi. He was now at Southwest Louisiana State.

The race got off to a slow start; no one had been racing in a long time. I didn't know what I could do because there hadn't been any way to test myself after the weather turned bad. I had set myself a goal for the race, however, and immediately took the lead, planning to go through two miles in nine minutes.

Through the first six laps I was on schedule and feeling very good. I thought to myself I should have started faster. Then, suddenly, I felt a pain in my right side. I was forced to slow down and massage my side. For three laps I continued to massage my side, but it got worse. I was forced to run in a bent position. I was actually jogging but all the other runners were content to stay behind.

After three laps of running in this awkward position the pain began to ease and with two laps to go I was feeling all right. They had missed their chance to take the lead from me for if the pace had been pushed the cramp would have remained and I would have had to drop out.

But now it was too late for them as I again started to pick up the pace. I had to be careful because I didn't want the cramp to return. I waited until the last 300 meters before I *really* started moving. With the last lap in 56 seconds, I easily won the race, beating Marin by four seconds.

On the way home the next morning, I thought the race wasn't too bad considering the trouble I had encountered. My time was 14:20. I wouldn't win any big races, but I was satisfied. Besides, it was December.

SEVEN

Running On The Boards

After two weeks of training in the cold I was entered in the Boston Knights of Columbus meet. My competition would come from Chris Williamson of Canada and Tom Laris. I had felt so good in the early stages of the Sugar Bowl meet, I decided to try again for a good mark.

There was no strategy. I took the lead at the gun and went through the two-mile in 9:00.7. Still, I felt good and kept up the pace for the next 440. Again I felt my side start to cramp as it had in New Orleans. I slowed the tempo slightly to relax the muscles and was again surprised when no one took the lead.

Finally, with 500 yards to go, Williamson passed me and I relaxed behind him. My side was better now and with 440 yards remaining, I sprinted into the lead. Laris had dropped off the pace and Willamson was my only worry.

With a last 440 in 58 seconds I beat the young Canadian by 40 yards and in the process broke the American record for the indoor three-mile. My time was 13:31.4, the second fastest three-mile ever run indoors. I felt good afterward and hadn't become overly fatigued. I thought to myself excitedly, "I could run a lot faster."

The West Coast meet directors wouldn't give me an invitation as yet and the meets in San Francisco and Los Angeles promised good competition. There was a new youngster from Washington, 18-year old Gerry Lindgren, who was thrilling the crowds.

People were starting to predict no other American would beat him over the two and three mile distance this year. That upset me but for now I had enough to worry about for I would soon be running against a man who would give me all the competition I needed. In fact, at the January 24 meet in Toronto there were two such runners.

Alby Thomas of Australia was coming to America with his outdoor season behind him and the Canadian Bruce Kidd would also run. Alby had all but predicted a world record three-mile before the race. The track was new and had very tight turns which made it more difficult for a tall man to run, but it also hindered Kidd. His choppy running style was better suited to more gentle turns.

I had new shoes for this race for my other indoor shoes had torn at Boston. I always wore Adidas but a new pair had not arrived, so I was wearing shoes from another company. Situated on each side of the shoe, just in back of the little toe, was an inflexible plastic guard. I hadn't worn the shoes but they felt comfortable when I put them on. I had no choice but to wear them, which turned into an agonizing situation.

Alby didn't waste any time and immediately took the lead. With his first mile in just over 4:24, he set a good pace. I felt good as I followed Kidd through the first mile but I could feel my feet becoming hotter with each lap. A pain grew on the outside of each foot where that hard, inflexible plastic was situated. I wondered if the others were feeling the turns as I was. They were just too sharp and my feet were sliding all over the place. At six laps Alby's pace hadn't slackened and he was starting to break contact with us.

I passed Kidd at that point but Alby was almost 70 yards in front, timed in 8:49. I led Kidd through in 8:58. Alby was on a 13:14 pace. Kidd and I were on a 13:27 pace but I wondered if I could hold it. As I looked toward Alby, running very relaxed, I thought he must be keeping up the tempo but there was no way of knowing.

The crowd, realizing the world record was an easy mark, had drowned out the times with their cheers. I only knew my feet were killing me; blisters had started to form and the plastic was cutting into my foot. How I wished the race was over so I could take off my shoes.

I could see Alby pulling away and wondered if he were tiring. I needed to go faster but my feet were so painful I couldn't. It became two races during the last mile. Alby against the clock and Bruce against me for second place. We both knew Alby couldn't be caught at this stage and we settled down to race one another.

Trying to ignore my agonizingly painful feet, I was still leading Bruce with a little more than 440 to go. The adrenaline was flowing now and I was doing a good job, almost forgetting about my feet, but if I was to take second I'd have to start my finish kick before Bruce since I knew his speed was equal to mine.

At one point in the race we had dropped more than 100 yards behind Alby but as we came into the last lap we had cut that distance considerably. Alby had used his energy in a concerted drive. But I wasn't much concerned about Alby now, for Kidd was at my shoulder when the last lap began. I could almost feel his breath on my neck as we moved down the back straight.

Coming off the final turn he challenged me but I had momentum and held him off by a couple of strides. Alby broke the world record in 13:26.4, and I beat Bruce by three-tenths of a second in 13:36.9.

The time was not nearly as fast as the Boston race but I had suffered much more. My feet were full of blisters and bleeding where the plastic had cut gashes. I wasn't the only one who had problems. Bruce and Alby both had tremendous blisters and I realized they also had felt pain. It was no wonder we had slowed during the last mile for it was then our feet were throbbing the most. Alby could have possibly run very close to 13:14 and Bruce and I could have come close or even broken the existing world record as well. When I talked to them afterward I could see fatigue wasn't the problem with any of us. We had to accept the fact that the track had been badly engineered and consequently we were the victims.

After flying back to Dayton, I rested on Sunday at my parents' home in West Milton. On Monday morning I drove the 60 miles to Sharon in Oxford, who as usual couldn't accompany me to the meet because of lack of funds. Sharon was very empathetic as I showed her my torn-up feet and was concerned about my resuming training.

The blisters were not so bad that I couldn't train; I just used dozens of Band-Aids. The cuts made by the plastic looked like someone had used a knife on my feet. It would heal quickly.

The next race was to be in New York on Friday so I didn't have a lot of time to rest. This, of course, was also true of most of the competition. The week passed quickly. I caught my plane at 2 p.m. and was in the hotel in New York city by 5 p.m. I had a couple of hours to rest before facing Bruce Kidd, Tom O'Riordan, and Pat Clohessy, the three main contenders in a field which also included Billy Mills, Tom Laris, Oscar Moore, and Pat Traynor.

Tom O'Riordan grabbed the lead and held it throughout the first two and one half miles. At that point Kidd took the lead, eventually winning in a fairly good time of 13:32.4. I had given it all I had with a 13:33.8, but it just wasn't enough. Bruce had turned the tables on me from the week before and beat me in almost the same way I had beaten him -- with a long finishing kick.

The next day I flew to Boston to run my first mile of the season as I decided I needed to work in some speed. I was a little tired from the night before and hoped to run the race on strength.

Thank goodness none of the big names were there as I was very tired soon after the start. Although I won, I wasn't satisfied with my 4:08.9 and had been completely fatigued at the end. I'm sure the three-mile race the night before was part of the problem. I decided I had better take it easier in my training during the new few days so I could recuperate for the *Los Angeles Times* meet on the West Coast the following weekend. There I'd be facing Ron Clarke of Australia in the two-mile. Ron was close to breaking records at 5000 and 10,000 meters and was a formidable opponent.

Stepping off the plane in LA, I made a quick call home to Sharon, who gave me her usual encouraging words. Out of the airport the weather was great. From the cold of winter I stepped into what seemed like summer. It was at times like these I regretted leaving the great training conditions of the West Coast.

I felt more rested now and thought of my 4:08 mile of the week before. I could stay close to Clarke even if he started in 4:16 for the first mile. I was confident I could give him a good race. Like Alby Thomas, Clarke was coming to the United States after his outdoor season and was ready for his best performances.

There was one advantage I had over him, however; I had run several indoor races and was more accustomed to them. Clarke had run a best of 8:35.2 during his outdoor season but that didn't bother me. I felt I was able to run faster than the 8:37 I had run the year before. Julio Marin and Ron Larrieu, another ex-teammate under Igloi, were also competing and I never discounted an Igloi man.

The arena was full with 13,000 people as we stepped onto the track. We were all introduced and received polite applause; that is, everyone except Ron Clarke, who was introduced last. I thought the roof was going to be lifted off the place. That sort of thing has a tremendous psychological effect on an athlete, and Clarke was no exception.

As the gun sounded Clarke sprinted into the lead with Larrieu in second and I followed Marin in fourth. Clarke led through splits of 63.5, 2:09.1, 3:15, and 4:21.1 for the first mile while the positions remained the same behind him. I found it awkward running behind such short men as Larrieu and Marin but I had to bide my time. Then Marin broke contact and I moved into third. Clarke continued to set the pace through a 67.5 fifth lap and 67.6 sixth lap.

With about 800 yards to go, I decided it would be easier to take the lead and be in the command position. I led through the seventh quarter in 66.3. One 440 to go now, not quite three laps of the indoor track. The tempo was picking up as I tried to shake Clarke, but he stuck to my heels. Larrieu was beginning to falter but was still in contention. With a lap of the small track remaining, I started sprinting but Clarke was still there. I was confident as I sprinted down the back stretch for I didn't think Clarke could match my speed.

It wasn't a fast last quarter mile, run in just under 60 seconds, but the real sprint hadn't started until 120 yards from the finish. It was good enough to win by six-tenths of a second and I had bested the man everybody said couldn't lose. The crowd went wild. I had set a stadium record at 8:42.2, and had a shot at the most valuable athlete award.

As the meet neared an end Tom O'Hara beat Jim Grelle in the mile in a very tactical 4:07. Now, I thought I had a real chance for the award because I was the only entrant to break a meet record. However, it was not to be and the award was given to Bill Crothers of Canada, who had placed second in the 1,000-yard dash. He had been beaten by Jim Dupree in a photo finish. But the reason he was voted the award was that during the early going he had gotten into a shoving match with another runner and had fallen. He jumped to his feet and almost caught Dupree at the tape. It was a tremendous performance, but still I was hurt and saddened by the vote of the sports writers.

On the long plane ride back to Oxford the next day I felt that the emotional aspect of Crother's effort had been taken too strongly. What if he hadn't fallen and then had won the race? Would they have voted him the outstanding performer? He would have had to run much faster to break the meet record. I called home and commiserated with Sharon about the award and the apparent unfairness of the choice. I didn't understand the sportswriters reasoning at all. Maybe it was a small thing but I wanted to be recognized when I ran well.

The next weekend was also going to be tough because I had two two-mile races. The first, and more challenging, was Thursday in New York at the Athletic Club meet. On Saturday I'd be in Louisville, Ky. For Thursday's race Kidd had rested the prior weekend and would be ready. Clarke was flying in from the West Coast and wouldn't want to lose two in a row. Also in the race were Clohessy, O'Riordan, and Laris.

During the first mile, Clarke and I exchanged the lead as we went through in 4:28. After that it was Clarke who set the tempo and Kidd moved into second. I was cut off and forced into fourth behind O'Riordan. It didn't matter at this point and I was satisfied with my position.

The positions remained the same through one and one half miles as Clarke continued to move away and Kidd followed. I moved past O'Riordan into third and soon after took the lead from Clarke. I led at one and three quarter miles in 7:45, but Kidd challenged on the next straight away and took the lead. He was trying to do what he had done in our last meeting but this time I was prepared.

I waited patiently on his shoulder as the pace quickened. We were coming down the straight with only one lap remaining and I could see Kidd watching me from the corner of his eye. Just as we were going into the final lap and the gun sounded, I sprinted all out. I had surprised Kidd, who never expected me to pass on the turn.

I was around him quickly and flying down the back straight. Kidd was on my shoulder and gaining. I decided to allow him to come up on my shoulder and then hold him off on the turn. This would force him to run a longer distance. Closer he came until he was even and as we went into the last turn our shoulders were touching.

He was giving it everything he had. He inched ahead, but not enough to cut in. I waited just a few strides more to give it all I had. The next moment, however, he moved in on me, cutting me off. I threw up my hands. I had to chop my stride, which caused me to lose momentum. There were only 40 yards to go now as I regained my balance and took out after him. Now I had to move to the outside as I began closing the gap.

At the tape I leaned but I could see I had missed. He had won, but surely he would be disqualified for the foul. The judges, however, had been blind and they let it go. The race was mine and I was angry. I knew, however, it would do no good to lodge a protest. It would only make it seem as though I was a sore loser. I wouldn't have minded if he had beaten me fairly, but not this way. However, I should have never allowed him to inch ahead of me on the turn.

I never blamed Bruce, because I knew he hadn't done it intentionally, but he should have been disqualified. Kidd had run 8:42.6 and I had run 8:42.8 with both of us running the last 440 in 57 seconds. Clarke was beaten for the second time in a row, finishing third in 8:43.8.

On Saturday I ran the race in Louisville where the competition was not as tough. I ended up winning with a time of 8:47.3 after pulling away in the last mile, running 4:19.5. The next day, I left with my parents, Sharon, and my brother, Dave, who had driven the 150 miles from home to see me run. As we went into a small restaurant one of the networks was showing the meet from New York on Thursday. It was upsetting to see the race and verify the foul had happened. My family was sympathetic, agreeing that the competitive world was certainly challenging and very complex. I guess that was one way of putting it.

By the end of the week, after I returned to Oxford, my classes, and training, I felt weak and ill. I had an inner ear infection and was put on antibiotics. The next weekend was the National Indoor Championship meet. I didn't have a sponsor and the AAU would not pay my way. They did pay for Ron Clarke, who broke the world record for three miles. It would have been nice to be in that race. On Thursday, February 27, I was still tired and on antibiotics when I flew to the New York Knights of Columbus meet in Madison Square Garden to run a mile.

As I warmed up for the race I knew it wasn't going to be a good evening. I never should have come. I was too tired and the competition was tough. I only placed third with a 4:07 time. I guess the time was fair, considering how poorly I felt. Tom O'Hara ran 3:58.5 and Canadian Ergas Leps was second in 4:03.6.

Upon returning home I knew I had to completely recover because I had a tougher race in Chicago just a week away. I didn't allow much time to rest, though, and through the weekend I trained fairly hard. I was feeling so tired on Monday that I went to the hospital for a blood test. The results came back with a diagnosis of anemia. My blood was 40 percent of normal. I received a B-12 shot and was put on iron. With only three days before the Chicago race, I didn't know if my body would recover enough.

On Wednesday and Thursday I took it easy in my morning and evening workouts and I did my usual pre-race workout on Friday morning. I caught a flight for Chicago that afternoon. By the time I arrived to warm up that night I was feeling much better. I thought about the competition of Peter McArdle, a tough runner, and Simo Saloranta, the Finnish champion, and Bruce Kidd, who would be my toughest opponent.

As it came time for the two-mile race, I made my way to the starting line and I thought back to my last race in this same arena. Jim Beatty had set a world record in the two-mile with 13,000 people giving all of us deafening applause. What a night that was. But now I had to concentrate on this race.

The gun sounded and the Finn jumped in front, opening a 40 yard lead with me in second at the three-quarter mark. Although somewhat lethargic, I felt in control and knew I could close the gap at any time. Then McArdle went by and upped the tempo. Within

440 yards we caught the Finn and McArdle went around him. Kidd slipped by me and also passed Saloranta but then the Finn fell into the tempo so I remained in fourth.

For the next few laps we ran in the same order in a tight group. I had been watching Kidd carefully and with four laps to go he jumped into the lead. I moved at almost the same instant, quickly passing the Finn and McArdle and within a few strides was immediately in back of Kidd. We pulled away from the others and I knew it would be a fight to the finish.

For two laps I stayed close on his shoulder, trying to relax as much as possible. My thoughts now were on when I should make the final move. I knew it would have to come as a surprise, my usual strategy with Kidd, and I pondered where to strike. Finally, there were two laps to go.

Before we went into the turn, I had made up my mind. I lifted my knees and drove as hard as I could. Within a step I was beside Bruce. I had indeed caught him by surprise and could see he couldn't recover in time.

Then a sharp pain. An elbow hit me in the side. But nothing could slow me down now. I was around him sprinting. There were only 200 yards to go, and it would be all out from here.

Bruce recovered quickly and was so close I could feel his breath. Around another turn I could see the gun raised for the final lap.

The gun fired as we went by and I drove even harder. Down the back straight Bruce moved even closer on my shoulder and we hit the final turn. I could hear the crowd now as the sound came in waves. In the middle of the turn we went, Bruce not giving an inch; it was going to be tight. About 60 yards remained and we were straining for the tape. Bruce had moved to the outside and I could see him out of the corner of my eye. Could I hold him off?

The line stretched out in front. With no more than a foot separating us we both drove hard, but I drove harder. My chest hit the finish line and I won. I knew it immediately. I had run 8:48.8, with the last quarter in 58 seconds. With all the problems I had been having, I felt great. I knew now it would only be a short time before I was completely recovered and would be running even faster.

It was later I remembered the last time I had raced Kidd he had accidentally fouled me and he hadn't been called for it. At least this time when I was hit with his elbow it didn't stop me. I had won a strategical race and I was satisfied.

With one week of training in front of me, I'd be running in Cleveland the following Saturday. The week went well and by Friday I felt much improved. I knew I'd be ready for a good run.

Arriving in Cleveland, I thought about the race and the articles in the newspapers. I was the clear favorite and was expected to win. That made the emotions tougher to control.

It is so much easier when you are the underdog. There is always the chance someone unknown will have a good night and upset things, especially if you're not feeling your best. I was almost the hometown boy as I stepped on the track.

Being a native of Ohio and having had a good indoor season, the crowd was pulling for an arena record, which was held by Laszlo Tabori. Laszlo had run 8:47.8 on this shorter, 12-lap track with a good performance, but I was determined to break the mark.

At the gun, Andy Schramn, my teammate at Miami, broke into the lead and continued to set the tempo (in the mid 4:20s) through the first mile. That pace was fine, but as he started slowing I assumed the lead.

At one and three-quarter miles I was 7:44.6, which was about what I had been doing in my other races. As I heard the time I knew I'd break the record as I only had to run a 62 in the last 440. I stepped up the pace.

As I came around with two laps to go, I glanced at the lap signs and saw the same number that was there before. What happened? Did the official forget to change the number or had he made a mistake in the early part of the race? I couldn't be sure. I was confused. My concentration was broken. I had to conserve energy.

I had intended to start sprinting on that lap but had to wait one more. Now the lap counter had two, and I started my sprint. I left all the others far behind and was running against the clock. There was no way the record of Tabori could stand.

As I crossed the finish line, there were cheers and applause from the crowd. I thanked them for their shouts and encouragement by jogging a lap around the arena. As I came by the timers, I was stunned when the official informed me my run was just over 9:11. I couldn't believe it. Obviously it was a mistake; I knew myself better than that. I knew I had run near the marks I had set earlier in the season.

When a time of 8:51.1 was officially announced, I knew that had to be wrong also. I approached the meet director to see what was happening. He explained that they thought we had run an extra lap, and the 8:51.2 was just a guess. If that were so, it meant I had run the last 440 in 66.6; I knew that was impossible. I was upset.

Later that evening several people informed me their watches had caught me between 8:41 and 8:42 with a lap to go. That was more like it, but I knew it would never be official. Who said trying to get to the Olympics would ever be easy?

I put all the negatives behind me as the indoor season ended and I considered it to be very successful since I had raced and beaten all the top distance runners except Gerry Lindgren and George Young. Now with the weather warming up, I could use the fields and track once again. I knew it was going to be a good year. A very good year.

EIGHT

The Spring of 1964

The week of March 16 I started hard training: the Olympics were looming closer. There had been mention in a few newspaper stories that I looked like a good bet to make the Olympic team in the 5000 meters.

It was too early to start worrying about whom I'd have to beat because the big names hadn't even begun to run yet. I'd just concentrate on pushing myself in a sensible training program hoping that when the time came I'd be ready.

But I assessed my competition early so I wouldn't have any surprises later. Beatty had cut his foot quite badly but was still training and thought he'd be ready for the outdoor season. Bill Dellinger was running again and I remembered back to the Air Force championship meet in Denver, when I had seen him win the steeplechase, the 1500 meters, and the three-mile with great ease. I knew he could be tough.

Of course, there was Gerry Lindgren -- young and brash, full of spirit with nothing to lose. I hadn't yet run against him but knew he'd have to be considered a tough contender as were Larrieu, Keith Foreman and Oscar Moore. I knew there would be others who would make themselves known during the outdoor season.

Four days had passed since my race in Cleveland and my training was hard and grueling. On Thursday night after my workout,

Coach Bob Epskamp asked me if I'd run on two relay teams in the Livingston Relays at Denison College. Though I was tired from training, I thought it would be a fun race and accepted his invitation. We won both our relays and I did have a lot of fun, although running on the small dirt track without the turns being banked had its challenges.

The next weekend I was to run a 3,000 meter race in San Diego. I'd be running against Dyrol Burleson, Tom O'Hara, and Jim Grelle, some of the top milers in the country. I wanted to run a fast time.

Weather conditions were terrible as we had 20 mile per hour wind gusts and the race became strategical. Dyrol and I were in the lead against the other two as the weather worsened and Dyrol ended up beating me by a yard in 8:06.9.

Considering the bad conditions I was very satisfied with second place and the fact that I could stay with the kick of one of the world's best milers.

As I thought about what I had just told myself, I had to smile inwardly. Even though I had lost the race and didn't like that aspect, I still found something positive to think about. There was no doubt I felt it was important to dwell on the positive and let the negatives be washed away. I had done it my entire life from the time I was young with my near-death experiences and chronic illness with asthma.

Many things could have stopped me if I had looked on the downside of circumstances and perpetuated the negative. I would never have gotten to this point of running with the greatest athletes in the world. It is important, of course, for healthy thinking to feel and discuss injustices and disappointments, but the mind takes in as many thoughts as it is given and we must let the negatives go as quickly as possible.

This includes, most importantly, self-esteem. All those disappointments in life are just that -- disappointments. They are not because "I am a bad person and deserve bad things to happen," but because that is the way life is. And if I'm positive about myself and let the negatives go, I can look to my next goal. People then may be happy to be around me and enjoy my company. I can bring a little something to them and they to me. Self-worth, believing in what I am doing and what I want to do; to be goal-oriented, to have progression in my life.

I was feeling good about my running and my progression was going along just fine. If nothing interfered, my positive attitude would remain strong. If something caused an erosion in the future I knew I would bring about a healing very quickly.

The next weekend, April 4, I traveled with the Miami team to the University of Kentucky Relays at Lexington and I got a chance sooner than I wanted to pull myself up once again.

Newspapers reported I was entered in the two-mile, but I heard Jim Murphy being told by his Air Force coach that the competition would not be good; that he could set the pace and go for a good time. Were they serious, I wondered, did they receive any sports news in Colorado? I decided right then and there to blow him away in the race.

I won in 8:47.5, the fastest time in the nation, and after the first lap he was no longer in the race. Sometimes another's negative attitude works into a positive for you if you let it.

Although this was a good race, I knew that only a few races had been run in the U. S. My real victory was that I had come very close to my personal best of the summer before and had set a new record for Miami.

The following week there was a dual meet between Miami and Bowling Green but I decided not to race in it because there had been some disagreement between Bob Epskamp and me. Instead I decided to put in a good week of training.

When I was racing every week I only trained hard on Monday and Tuesday. But now, after a light jog on Sunday to rest my body from the race, I put in two very good days, took it easy on Wednesday, and came back with a hard day on Thursday. I could really feel the speed coming in my legs. The week of hard work was just what I needed and winter had finally broken. I wanted to use these good days to full advantage.

On Thursday evening, just as I was finishing my workout, I was visited by George Rider, my old coach, and my ex-teammate, Dick Clevenger. Both were good friends and I respected them highly. They had heard I decided against running in the dual meet because of this squabble with Coach Epskamp and wondered if I was doing the wise thing. They said there was more at stake than just proving I was my own man.

We talked for quite a while that evening and I told them of my hard workouts and their value. Coach Rider said that was fine but he insisted it would hurt the program if I didn't run. After listening to them I took a deep breath and sighed; I knew they were right. I had been out of line. I would run. But if I was to take part I wanted it to be something that would bring out interest in Miami track.

Later that evening I went to Rick Cunningham's room and asked him if he would be willing to help me during the first part of the mile. After telling him what I wanted to do, he agreed; I trusted him to do a good job.

There was one other problem. The maintenance people hadn't placed the cinder track in proper order and the first lane was loose with excessive cinders. On Friday morning, I asked the coach if he could have the track raked and rolled, explaining what I had in mind. Together we went to Athletic Director Dick Shrider, who assured us he'd have workers on it that afternoon. I volunteered to help out in any way I could and said I'd be out there at 2 p.m. Everything was arranged. My plan was to break the four-minute mile the next day.

At 2 p.m. I was at the track, alone. I found a wheelbarrow and shovel and started to manicure the first lane, raking and smoothing it for the next day. I removed seven loads of loose cinders that had been washed onto the lane by the spring rains. Three freshman runners had come to help carry the last loads away; it looked pretty good when we finished. Feeling a little stiff in the shoulders, I walked back to my apartment. I was upset that the maintenance men hadn't shown. I let it go by the time I reached home, and that evening, after jogging easily, the stiffness went away. I was ready for tomorrow.

The next morning I awoke to a beautiful spring day and the return of a little stiffness in my shoulders. I went to the grass field to loosen up and felt pretty good when I returned home for breakfast.

As the meet was under way that afternoon we knew it would be close because the teams were evenly matched. Race after race was exciting and the stands were filled with more people than I had ever seen at a Miami dual meet. Rick told me he had spoken about the race to a few of his many friends. I was excited as I warmed up and anxious to get started. Thirty minutes before the race I told Rick what I wished him to do.

"Rick, the first lap is yours," I explained. "I don't want to worry about it at all. We'll go through the first 440 in 57 seconds, no slower. Do you think you can do it?"

"I'll do it," he answered.

Looking into his eyes I could see he, too, was excited about the race, and because there was no competition from Bowling Green, it was a perfect situation.

"If you can keep up the pace after the first lap, go ahead and do it, OK?" He nodded in agreement. I placed my hand on his shoulder and said, "Let's give it a try."

Word of our intentions had spread and as the call came for the mile, the stands were buzzing. I removed my warm-ups and walked to the line, nervous, but relaxed. Clevenger, who was the official starter that day, gave me a pat as he walked by. This was it: what I hoped would be my first sub four-minute mile.

We stood at the line receiving last-minute instructions from Clevenger. I really wasn't listening to what he was saying but was concentrating on the job ahead. My adrenaline was beginning to flow as I allowed my body to become excited. Clevenger walked to the side of the track and turned to ask the timers if they were ready.

"Runners, set!" he shouted.

I could see Rick tensing for the gun and then it sounded. Rick jumped into the lead and I was by the other runners to move in behind him. We started fast and were around the first turn and into the back straight. I was running on his shoulder and the tempo felt good. We moved around the far turn and into the straight. I could see the fans on their feet and my concentration broke momentarily as their cries carried to me. We were then at the first-quarter mark and the timer yelled the split as we went by.

"Fifty-seven!" he shouted. Right on schedule. Around the turn and into the back straight again, but I could feel that Rick was slowing.

"Faster!" I yelled.

Rick immediately upped the tempo. Coming into the half-mile

now, Rick was beginning to slow again and I knew it would do no good to shout. Before it had been a mental lapse, but now he was feeling fatigue. Rick remembered that I had told him to move into the second lane and allow me to remain in the first lane, passing him on the inside.

"Good job!" I said as I passed him. At the halfway point the timer shouted, "1:57!" I was satisfied and felt strong. Rick was dropping back rapidly now. I could no longer hear his footsteps. I was on my own. This was the crucial lap. If I could hold the tempo, I would be fine. On the back straight I kept thinking of my speed.

"Don't daydream now!" I reprimanded myself

Around the turn I could see Clevenger standing in the middle of the track with the starting gun in the air. I was tiring but knew I could still give it a good finish. One more lap to go and 2:59 was yelled as I passed. A few more steps and Dick fired the pistol.

I could hear the people again in the stands. They were going wild. I had never heard so much noise at a Miami track meet before. My legs still felt good as I headed into the back straight for the last time. Then my shoulders: I couldn't relax them.

"Relax!" I commanded them but as I went into the final turn, running with everything I had, I couldn't gather myself. I couldn't change over into a sprint because I needed to be relaxed to do that. My body was feeling the effect of my shoulder muscles tightening and although I was holding my tempo, I was beginning to struggle.

Eighty yards to go now and I drove with everything I had. I was fighting myself as the tape loomed just 10 yards away! Through it I went and it was over. I dropped my arms. Oh, they were aching.

For the moment I wasn't interested in the time. My shoulders felt as if someone had given me a beating. Clevenger was the first to come to my side. There were no words, just a pat on the back. It was all that was needed. I turned around to see Rick finish in second in a good time of 4:07. The crowd was silent as the timers studied their watches. Rick and I were jogging as we both waited for the official announcement.

Finally over the loudspeakers came the results:

"In first place, with a new Miami and a new field record, with a time of four...," the voice droned on. I wasn't listening. I wanted to cry. I had it at the three-quarters mark and let it get away. Anger welled up in me as I thought of the day before and the promise of help with the track; it wasn't fair. It was going to be tough letting the negatives go on this one. Then the announcement was repeated:

"Bob Schul has just run the fastest time ever in the state of Ohio. His 4:00.9 mile breaks the mark of the great Gunder Haegg, who ran 4:05.4 some 20 years before."

I was still disappointed, so very disappointed. As Rick and I jogged in front of the main stands the crowd rose to its feet and cheered. I looked up and saw Sharon smile at me. What a wonderful crowd I thought, and I waved back in response. My teammates offered their congratulations, as did Coach Rider, Dick Clevenger, and Bob Epskamp. With all this great support, I was feeling much better. After all, it hadn't been a bad race.

As the competition continued, the schools were locked in a classic battle. The mile relay would decide the meet. Since I had been on the mile relay team as a sophomore and had run a split of 48.8 several years earlier, I approached Bob Epskamp and asked if he wanted me to run. I had completely recovered from the mile and knew I could run faster than in my earlier years. He turned me down, stating the regular team could win the race. OK, I thought as I walked away, you're the coach. Well, 3:15.6 later he was proven wrong. Bowling Green won the race and the meet.

The next weekend I was going to the Kansas Relays to run in a 10,000 meter race. I had wanted to try the distance and when they called with the invitation, I readily accepted. The 10K was to be held on Friday night with the main meet on Saturday. I flew out on Thursday and was picked up at the airport and taken to a dormitory to spend the night. The next afternoon I went to the track to start my warm-up and began to wonder if the race had been canceled as there was no one in the stands. The officials assured me everything was fine and the race would start on schedule.

There were only six of us running and John Macy from the University of Houston was one of the best 10K runners in the U. S. although he was an Australian citizen. During my warm-up the wind picked up and dust was being blown around. I could feel a change in my body and my throat was becoming a little sore. This could not be good, I thought.

As the race got under way I assumed the lead and traded with

Macy over the first nine laps. After that I fell off the pace as Ireland Sloan of Kansas Teachers College passed me. With the wind gusting to 20 mph and the 82 degree temperature, not to mention my allergies, I was not having a fun time. With a mile to go Ireland stepped off the track, stating later he had cramps. I must admit the same thoughts went through my mind but I knew I could finish the last mile. Macy ran well, finishing in 29:49. My second place was 30:15. It would be good to return to Ohio.

The following weekend, April 25, the team went to the Drake Relays in Iowa but I went to the Mt. SAC Relays in Walnut, California to run the 5000. Considering the poor condition of the track I was very satisfied with my time of 13:59.4. I led most of the race and pulled away in the last mile. Billy Mills finished second in 14:09.4.

Friends usually put me up when I went to California because it was hard to make ends meet, especially without a scholarship. Sharon was still making $200.00 a month. Money was scarce. She was really wonderful about all my traveling and the insufficiency of funds for her to come along. Sharon understood our financial dilemma and told me that instead of dwelling on my being gone she used the time to her advantage, catching up on her reading and visiting friends.

When I arrived home from California the next day I started thinking of my chances of making the Olympic team. Although I was confident I could make the team at 10,000 meters, or even the steeplechase, I would go at 5000 meters only. It was my best race. I told a sportswriter for the Dayton, Ohio, *Journal Herald* that if I didn't make the team I should be kicked all the way across the country.

My thinking had changed from just a few months before when I thought I had some chance to make the team. Now my racing had proven to me that making the team was a conclusive fact. I finally had all the confidence I needed and once again I assessed my journey.

I now fully believed in myself. It was a long, gradual process that came one small step at a time. It wasn't enough that I just mouthed the words. I had to believe, deep within my soul, completely. I dispersed all doubts and replaced them with the knowledge that what I had done to prepare myself had placed me in a position where I knew I could overcome any obstacle. I found ways to build a solid wall of knowledge, confidence, and self-esteem; and if that wall should become cracked within the final months of preparation, I could repair it quickly with my strongest block. That block, the one that I mention so often in this writing: the resurgence of positive thinking and its domination over self-doubt.

I was ready to attempt my boyhood dream to be special in something, to be great at it, to have my family proud of me, to prove to them that I wasn't a weakling just because I had been sickly. I wanted so badly to do this, not just for them, but for myself as well.

Winning the one mile race for west Milton in the 1955 Dayton district championships.

West Milton Cub scout pack, circa 1945 (above). I'm third from the left in the back row.

Running the two mile race for Miami U. in the 1964 New York Athletic Club's event in Madison Square Garden. Back of Schul is Tom Larris, Tom O'Riordan of Ireland and Ron Clark of Australia (below).

The super coach, Mihaly Igloi, who often ran 13 rugged training sessions a week (above).

In international competition, a steeplechase in 1961 in Brussels (above).

Setting the American 5000 meter record in 1964 at the Compton, California Invitational. Bill Baillie of New Zealand is second. Last lap was run in :54. (right)

Winning the 5000 meter Olympic trials in 1964 in Los Angeles (above).

Norpoth of Germany, Schul and Dellinger after the medal ceremony in Tokyo

Overtaking Billy Mills, who won the 10k gold in Tokyo, on the way to a 2-mile world record at Pierce Junior College. George Young at left (above).

Finish of world record 2 mile, 8:26.4, Second Billy Mills 8:45.6 (left).

Mom and Dad on the way to Alaska, over the North Pole, to Tokyo (above).

West Milton throws a welcoming parade. West Milton had a population of 1800 people and 5000 people attended the homecoming.

Also on hand to greet Sharon and Bob at their triumphal homecoming was Ohio Governor James Rhodes (above). Later, Bob was given the Governor's Award for outstanding achievement; other honorees that year included Dr. Albert Sabin and Raymond Firestone.

A rare moment of relaxation after competing in Hawaii in 1965.

Bob at age 50 is finishing a half marathon in 1hour 16 minutes while training 45 miles a week.

NINE

Overcoming Obstacles

Deciding to relax a little, which was really unusual for us, Sharon and I accepted a dinner invitation from our friends, Bill Gordon and his wife. Bill was working on his doctorate degree at Miami and lived on the outskirts of Oxford. Sharon and I decided on minimal discussion of running and just to enjoy each other's company.

The Gordons, and their two large Labrador Retrievers, greeted us warmly. They seated us in their livingroom and the dogs were very friendly with us, wagging their tails, wanting to be patted, etc. Bill and his wife brought out a cheese ball and crackers, and we were sipping wine and enjoying ourselves as our hosts disappeared for a moment into the kitchen. Before we knew it one of the dogs whisked over to the coffee table and started licking the cheese ball. I chased him away but the damage had been done. We looked at each other and Sharon said, "Should we tell them the dog licked the cheese?"

"No, no, we'd better not. Their feelings will be hurt," I answered.

Bill then came back in and asked if we wanted some more cheese.

"Oh, no," we said. "We want to save room for dinner."

Then Bill's wife came back in and started chatting away as they picked up the crackers, ready to use them for the cheese ball. Could I keep silent? The meal was delicious and we enjoyed their company on one of the few occasions I wasn't involved with my running.

My next race wasn't until May 9 when we met with Northern Illinois University so I had a lot of time for hard training. As always, one never knows what pitfalls will happen next. As you now know, supreme demands are placed upon the body. On one of those days, I decided to train at the track with the team. About an hour into the workout, as I was starting on my tenth 440, a sharp pain hit my knee. I yelled and pulled quickly to a stop. I was helped onto the infield by Dick Clevenger. The pain subsided, but when I got to my feet and tried to jog, the pain forced me to stop.

I went into the training room, but there was nothing the trainers could do. I'd just have to rest it for a couple of days to see what would happen. I remembered how it had been in past years when, as I reached my top conditioning, something would go wrong. Here it was again.

I only did light jogging for the next two days; then mysteriously, on the third day, the pain was gone as quickly as it had come. It was as if nothing had ever been wrong. What a relief. The next day I went back to my regular workouts with a great weight lifted from my mind. It was strange indeed, but I never did concern myself about it returning.

May 9 and the dual meet with Northern Illinois was fast approaching. It was also the date of the Miami Relays where high schools from all over the state send teams to compete. Because the setting was good and the biggest crowd of the year would be there, I decided to give the four-minute mile another try.

That week one of the Dayton newspapers sent a reporter to the campus and I told him my plans. I always let the media know what I planned to put added pressure on myself. I had chosen a bad time to try for the barrier, however, as the track was in bad shape from all the high school races. I ran 4:03.6. As Sharon and I drove home, I was very disappointed in myself and the fact that I had let the crowd down.

The next weekend I was to take part in the Coliseum Relays in Los Angeles. Once again I wanted to run the mile to try to break the four-minute barrier, and I was more concerned with breaking the magic mark than winning. Well, maybe slightly more. There would be tough competition, such as John Camien of Kansas State Teachers College; Paul Schlicke of Stanford; along with Bob Grelle and Bob Seaman, former teammates on the LA Track Club. Camien liked to lead in his races and I was hoping he would do the same in this race. I wanted to follow and have a big finish. I thought that way I was sure to break four minutes.

Unfortunately and with great frustration, I came in third with a time of 4:01.6. My strategy had gone as planned until the last 220 yards. Grelle was on Camien's shoulder and Schlicke had moved to the outside of the first lane. I ran to his inside, just behind. With 220 yards to go, Grelle made his move, just what I had been waiting for. I was ready to run. But in that instant when Grelle moved I expected Schlicke to take off, too. He didn't, and I was trapped. I had been foolish to run inside and it cost me another good chance at breaking four minutes. Camien won in 4:00.7 and Grelle followed in 4:01.4. I felt so stupid and frustrated at my misjudged strategy that I took it out on Schlicke as he came across the finish line. I yelled at him, "Why the hell didn't you move?"

The other athletes looked at me, and I turned away. I was so angry at myself but knew it was unfair to take it out on Schlicke. That night after due apologies and a couple of beers I forgot about the race and enjoyed the friendship of the other athletes and their wives and girlfriends. There would be another day.

Although my optimism was high the following weekend during the Mid-American Conference championships and my teammates did an excellent job of placing second in the team standings, I was tired and once again destined to be disappointed. I won the mile, but with a slow 4:07. My three-mile was also poor because of cramping in my side, but I won in 13:52.5.

The following week was the Ohio AAU championships in Dayton, only 20 miles from my home town. I wanted to continue on my speed work by breaking the meet record for the mile.

Soon the starter called us to our marks. We were off! My first lap went in 58 seconds, and I left the rest far behind. I felt good but with no competition it was tough trying to push myself. The 880 was just over two minutes, so I had slowed. I must push the third lap. I wasn't concentrating, and my relaxation was gone as I came around the turn into the gun lap.

The gun fired and I heard a split of 3:04. There was no way I was going to run below 56 by myself, especially since I'd been working hard on the first three laps. I tried to pick up the pace but wasn't very successful.

Coming into the tape I knew it was a good race but the four-minute barrier had eluded me again. There was no excuse except that my concentration and relaxation were off. I won in 4:03 by over 100 yards. Running that fast proved my condition was excellent. I was excited and ready for the big weekend coming up, the Compton Invitational.

The school year was over and Sharon and I were preparing to go to California for the entire summer so I'd have all the proper conditions for training. She was as excited as I was as we packed our belongings. Our plans were to leave for LA on May 21 so I would have plenty of rest for the big meet at Compton. Later in June we'd have to go to the East Coast on our way to the national championships and the first Olympic trials. We'd then return to the West Coast for further training and a shot at the final team in September.

We flew into Los Angeles planning to rent the inexpensive furnished apartment I had lived in as a bachelor. We used to call the place the "green monster" because it was furnished with a hodgepodge of cheap furnishings. It still looked the part. There was no choice but to take it for we couldn't afford anything else. I was only getting a per diem from the meet director, only enough for one person. Since we were used to being frugal, we managed fairly well. Also, a real plus was that the track Igloi used for morning workouts was close by at Dorsey High School.

After we were settled in, I went for my first workout early Monday morning. Igloi and his boys were there.

"Hi, Coach!" I said enthusiastically as I approached. It was good to see him after all this time.

"Bob! How are you?" he asked as he extended his hand, squeezing with strength from his gymnastic training as a youth in Hungary.

"Are your boys in top shape?" I asked as I tried to make small talk. I knew he would never meaningfully answer that question.

"Oh, they are all right," he said with a smile.

I knew they'd be in the best shape possible. "Well, guess I'd better get into it," I said as I moved away at a slow jog.

Soon I was into my full workout. That afternoon and the following day I did hard workouts, then lightened the load on Wednesday and Thursday. Day after day I could feel Igloi's eyes piercing through me, evaluating my condition. He was still the master and I knew he could sense what I felt in myself. I was ready.

After working hard all week, I needed to rest, relax, and have some fun visiting friends. Because the buses were on strike, we discovered a fun way to travel. We decided to buy a motor scooter. We looked in the papers, and after a phone call and our one and only taxi ride, we had our own transportation, all within two hours. Now we could go any place we wanted. Sharon rode on the back as I wove in and out of traffic. We had fun that week, visiting our friends as we had planned, going for walks, and just enjoying buzzing around town.

On Friday morning after training with Igloi, I did a very light workout. I jogged a mile and then went into a typical Igloi pre-race schedule, doing three sets of 10 times 100 meters. The first set was easy, not more than a jog, and after walking a 220 I did the next set at "fresh speed," which is relaxed running. The third set was what Igloi termed "shake up," a slow jog, shaking the arms loose. As I was doing these, I looked over and could see him smiling. Yes, it was still his training. I felt so good inside, so very good. When I reached the apartment, I wrote in my workout book that I could run 13:40, or if I were really pushed, a little below.

That afternoon I jumped on the scooter and drove to the hotel where most of the athletes were staying. It was something to do just to keep busy. I spent an hour visiting with the other runners who were competing that night. Soon it was time to return to the apartment for my pre-race meal and rest prior to heading for Compton.

Tom Rodda and his wife picked us up at the apartment that evening and we drove to Compton in time to see some of the races before warming up. It was a beautiful night, cool enough so that breathing wouldn't be a problem. I always warmed up alone for the big competitions for I wanted to set my own speed and didn't want to talk to anyone. It was 50 minutes before the race and I started to jog easy. Fifteen minutes passed when all of a sudden I started to get a cramp in my side. It wasn't hurting yet but I could feel the tightness and knew that under stress it would become serious. I thought about the other races where this had happened to me. I decided to do something about it instead of getting overly upset.

I went to the training tables at the far end of the field and found the man for whom I was looking, Stubb Evans, who worked with Dr. Dooley in Pomona. Stubb had loosened me up before in competition when I was in Los Angeles and he always did a magnificent job. I didn't want a rubdown, but asked if he could just work the spasm out. He twisted me first one way and then the other, working on my back. I could feel the vertebrae popping back into line as he manipulated, and a few minutes later he assured me there would be no more cramping. There was no tightness. Everything felt loose and relaxed.

"Thanks, Stubb," I said as I pulled on my sweat pants.

"Run a good one," he said.

There were 20 minutes to go before the race and I did a few sprints back and forth on the infield. I felt so good that I smiled to myself and went back to jogging. I began noticing the other competitors in the infield.

First there was Bruce Kidd, my nemesis from the indoor season and holder of the record for the fastest 5,000 meters ever run on American soil. Jim Beatty was doing sprints similar to mine, since we had been taught by the same man. Jim was always a threat. He held the U. S. record for 5 000 meters and had recently run 8:41 for the two-mile at the California Relays. He had been out-sprinted in that race by New Zealander Bill Baillie, the third entry who had run 8:37.1 to out-sprint both Kidd and Beatty. If he could beat Kidd on the sprint then I knew he had speed, for I vividly remembered my indoor races against Kidd.

There was young Gerry Lindgren, a high school boy from the state of Washington, who had made quite a name for himself since January. In fact, a sportscaster was sent from his home town to do a live account of Gerry and the race. I had been wanting to race him for a long time.

The other younger athletes included Julio Marin, Danny Murphy and Chris Williamson, none in Gerry's class. Lastly, there was the Igloi stable: the unpredictable Ron Larrieu, who could run a top race or be well off the pace. I wondered what he would do tonight. Also, there were his teammates, Tom Rodda and Bob Seaman. There were 12 of us, constituting at the time the best field ever to run the 5000-meter distance in the U. S.

A capacity crowd of 7,700 people in the small Compton High School stadium made a lot of noise. The race prior to the 5000 ended as I finished tying my spikes. The public address announcer was calling us to the starting line. I took off my warm-up clothes and tested the clay-cinder track. It was in beautiful condition, and again, I thought how perfect the night was for running. They called us to the starting line for introductions and we were presented to the crowd. Kidd, Baillie, Beatty, and Lindgren received big ovations as each took a few strides forward as his name was announced.

Finally, we were ready to go and the starter gave his final instructions. The gun was in the air.

"On your marks!" The gun sounded.

Kidd and Lindgren raced for the lead while the rest of us jockeyed for a good position. We had to be careful of each other's sharp spikes, a half inch long to grip the track. Lindgren took the lead on the inside with Kidd on his outside shoulder going around the first turn.

Down the back straight Kidd dropped back slightly as Lindgren poured it on. Coming into the first lap, the tempo was fast.

"Sixty-two!" yelled the timer, as the leaders went by. I was back in seventh position, very relaxed and heard, "Sixty-four!" I knew two seconds didn't separate us.

Kidd was making a bid for the lead now, and in his choppy style he was around Lindgren, but Lindgren was back on his shoulder. Beatty, looking heavy, was running third with Baillie a step behind. On his shoulder was Larrieu with Williamson tucked in close. I followed Williamson as closely as I dared. It was so crowded everyone had to be very careful of the others' spikes, but the pace felt good.

We were coming into the straight, which would be the finish eleven laps from now, and Lindgren was challenging Kidd again.

He would get a half-stride on Kidd, then Kidd would pick up the pace. Around the turn and into the half mile. It was 2:08 for the leader. On we went with Lindgren on Kidd's shoulder; the three quarters in 3:14 and the mile in 4:21.

I was still in back, but in contact and running smoothly. After the mile I moved up to sixth as Williamson allowed too much distance between himself and Larrieu. The race was among the six of us, running within six yards of each other, and the pace was on world record time. If this kept up someone would have to break soon, or did they all feel as good as me? A few more laps and we'd find out.

Beatty was running between Kidd and Lindgren during the fifth lap. It looked as if they were two chariot horses and he was handling the reins. Baillie, his shoulders held high, wasn't leaving any extra room between himself and Beatty, while Larrieu and I were breathing down his neck. The pace slowed in the fifth lap as we ran 68, and it gave everyone a chance to relax. I wasn't thinking of breaking any records. I wanted to win and was content to remain in sixth for the time being.

On the sixth lap Kidd again picked up the pace with a 67, but still the five of us were with him. On the seventh lap Kidd really slowed as he started to use tactics. It was the slowest lap of the race, 70 seconds, but we weren't going to continue with that tempo.

As Kidd started into the turn he again picked up the pace. On the backstretch he tried to break away. Lindgren stayed with him but Beatty fell back, breaking contact, which meant I had also broken contact. As soon as I saw what had happened I moved to the outside and passed Larrieu, then Baillie, and in a few strides, I passed Beatty. I closed on Lindgren and Kidd and by the turn had pulled up to them. Baillie and Larrieu also passed Beatty and followed me.

For two laps we ran in that order with Kidd going through the two-mile in 8:53. I was only a stride back now and feeling very comfortable and confident. After two and one-quarter miles I began considering taking the lead. It would have its advantages at this point, for I would have command.

Kidd had been doing what he wanted, now it would be my turn. A 220 went by and we had exactly three laps remaining. I swung wide, and picking up the tempo, moved to Lindgren's shoulder. I looked at him as I went by and then, just as easily, I passed Kidd. I increased the tempo to see what would happen. Beatty was the first to go as he dropped out. Later, Jim said a calf injury from the week before had tightened.

We were running 65-second quarters now and the positions were changing quickly in back of me. Larrieu moved into second with Kidd, Baillie, and Lindgren following. On the 11th lap, Baillie started moving up to prepare for his attack. Lindgren was moving into third, passing Larrieu, while Kidd was rapidly failing back.

Coming out of the turn after completing 11 laps, Baillie was right in back of me while Lindgren and Larrieu were falling back. It was a two-man race now. I knew that and I'm sure Bill knew it, too. The others had lost contact and would be unable to move in again.

Down the straight we came. I could see the pistol raised in preparation for the shot signalling the final lap.

Finally I could hear the crowd. They were yelling wildly and for the first time in the race, a trace of fear came to me. My mind was racing as much as I was. I mustn't lose. I can't. Past the line the gun fired. Adrenaline poured into my system. I glanced to the right to be sure Baillie wasn't going to make a sudden move on the turn. All I could see was his shadow being thrown on the track by the stadium lights.

Around the turn, and the lights were such that his shadow was there. I could sense him on my shoulder but the shadow told me he wasn't making a move, not yet. If his shadow moved to the outside I would know he had moved into the second lane, but all through the turn it remained in the same position. I was safe for now.

I thought about starting my finish. I knew Baillie had a good finish; I waited. We were half way through the turn now, picking up the pace slightly, but not sprinting. Around the turn and coming into the back straight, the shadow disappeared. The lights were at a different angle now.

My senses said "GO!" In a single stride I brought my knees high and was higher on my toes. I was a sprinter now. The strength was there. Baillie wasn't important. I was against myself. How fast could I run? If Baillie could sprint faster, it would be his race. All the tactics were over. The race would go to the fastest finisher.

I was moving as fast as I possibly could and was still relaxed. I could see the tape for the three-mile at the end of the straight. Baillie wouldn't beat me there. He must not. There was little fatigue as yet but I could feel it building. Sprinting always built it fast. Maybe I started too early. Was Baillie laying back for a final surge?

I drove past the three-mile mark and into the final turn. I loved being out front. I could hear the crowd again and I tried to drive harder. Out of the turn and down the final straight. I could see the finish line stretched across the track. I couldn't hear Baillie. Where was he? Was he closing? I must drive harder. Harder!

Thoughts raced through my mind. I mustn't lose! Closer, I came. Closer. My legs were tying up now but it didn't matter. My momentum would carry me through.

Twenty yards now and I hadn't slowed. Baillie wouldn't beat me now; I knew it, but I still drove as hard as I could. I hit the finish line, my face contorted from the 54.6 final lap. I was happy. The race had been easy up to the final lap. I could run even faster; I knew it. Much faster.

The time was announced a few minutes later. An American record for 5000 meters at 13:38 and the fastest time in the world so far that year. It was only three seconds off the world record. I knew at that moment I would be a contender at Tokyo. I was a happy man!

TEN

The Magic Four-Minute Mile

The next weekend, on June 13, there was a meet in San Diego, and wanting to go after the four-minute mile again, I entered. The men to beat were Cary Weisiger, who had run 3:58.9 at Compton, and Jim Grelle who had run 3:58.1.

Both had plenty of speed but I thought I could make a race of it and was most eager to break the four-minute barrier. If I lost the race but still ran a good time, I'd be satisfied; but I was still planning to win and would drive myself unmercifully to do it.

I hated losing with a passion.

After relaxing and training for a week in Los Angeles, Sharon and I flew down to San Diego on Friday. The race was on Saturday evening. I knew my condition was excellent and my plan was to force the pace in order to run a good time. After a good nights sleep I did a light workout Saturday morning and felt ready.

The evening was cool and beautiful when I arrived at the San Diego track. My race would be run at 8 p.m. so I was able to watch a few of the other races before warning up.

The most interesting race to me was the two-mile, for entered were many of the athletes who would be my competition in upcoming meets. The race was no surprise as Jim Beatty won in 8:38.4, pulling away in the final 200 meters from Tom Rodda. I smiled as he jogged around the track to the applause of the crowd, enjoying his showmanship. He was so confident and self-assured. I smiled again as I thought how confident I was about my ability. It was vital to be confident but it was important for it to be controlled confidence.

As we started to warm up for the mile, Grelle told me he was having a migraine headache and didn't think he'd run. Jim and I were close from the years of training under Igloi and I'd seen these severe attacks come on when he was under tension. He would become ill in just a few minutes and he would often vomit. In the past, when he thought the attacks weren't so severe, he would still run. But this attack was a bad one, and he had to withdraw. Now I had Cary and an Englishman, Peter Keeling, in the race as my stiffest competition. Without Jim I knew the pace would falter.

My thoughts now returned to the race because this could be my best opportunity to break the coveted four-minute barrier. I remembered when Roger Bannister broke the four-minute mile for the first time in England in 1954 when I was a junior in high school.

At that time I had no concept of what it meant or that one day I would be attempting the same feat. It was exciting to me as I warmed up for this race, for I fully expected to run faster than four minutes; knew that I could if only the pace would be fast enough in the early laps.

As I continued to jog I thought about my attempt to break the barrier a month earlier. Psychologically, my attitude was strong, but at times I still had trouble with breathing. But now, in California with this beautiful weather and the better track, I knew my time would be three to four seconds faster than any race I could run in Ohio.

When the gun sounded a local half-miler jumped into the lead with Cary in second and me in third. The first lap was fast enough, about 58 seconds. Coming past the starting line I moved into the lead. I felt better now after starting out somewhat sluggishly. My muscles were much looser and we covered the 880 in two minutes flat.

Weisiger moved to the front and set the pace. He moved strongly on the back straight, holding the 62 pace; we reached the three-quarters in 3:02. If I were to break the barrier I would have to move. I tried to pass Cary as we went into the back straight, but he held me off. Coming into the final turn, I dropped back so as not to run on the outside.

As we came off the turn I gathered myself for the final effort. I moved into the second lane and slowly began inching my way to Cary's side. With 50 meters to go, I was in front and started gradually pulling away. I was in an all-out sprint, ahead by three or four yards as I came to the finish.

Eagerly I awaited the announcement and then it came. I had run under four minutes for the mile. I ran 3:59.1 to Cary's 4:00. Anxiously I looked toward Sharon in the stands, and she waved excitedly to me for the joy of the moment. All along, since early spring, I knew it was only a matter of having a good track with the right competition.

When they came together the breaking of the four-minute mile was inevitable. I had done it and was satisfied. I thought I'd be happier than I was, but now it seemed anti-climatic. Nevertheless, I had joined an exclusive club and had beaten one of America's premier milers in the process.

ELEVEN

The Big Meets

It would seem at this point that relaxation be in order, but in striving toward the Olympics there was no time. The most important meets were still ahead and it was critical not to miss any training days. The next day we drove to LA with the Grelles and again resumed our hard workouts.

I decided not to run in the NCAA Championships although I was favored to win the 5000-meters. My decision meant that I would never run in an NCAA track and field meet. I had two important meets within a week and the NCAA's lack of competition didn't interest me.

The only thing on my mind was an Olympic victory in Tokyo and I wasn't going to let anything interfere with that goal. Perhaps I was a bit brash and egotistical. As the years have gone by, I regret not running.

The first big race coming up was the AAU Championships. The team to meet the USSR would be chosen from this race. Also looming were the first Olympic trials.

The races were close together and the location on the East Coast was not the best. Hot, humid weather meant trouble with my allergies. I wasn't looking forward to the trip and prayed that the pollen wouldn't affect me too much. I knew I would have to be extra careful.

I wasn't given much of a chance to worry about myself, though, because of the wonderful people of West Milton. I had stopped in my hometown because the people there wanted to give me a send-off for the two big meets in the East. I could lay-over without extra cost from the airlines since Dayton was not out of the way. For a town of only 3,000 people, it was really something.

When Sharon and I stepped off the plane, a band and many well-wishers met us at the airport and the mayor handed me the key to the city. It was such a warm feeling to have such kindness from my home town folks. This was the nice kind of pressure that made me want to win all the more.

After spending the night with my parents, I flew to Trenton, New Jersey, for the meet at nearby Rutgers University. My sponsor was the Dayton Athletic Club. I stayed with my friend, Jerry Foster, who lived near the university. Sharon and my mom were driving to meet me.

After reminiscing with Jerry, he told me of a place close to the apartment where I could jog. It would have been nice to become accustomed to the heat and humidity but I knew it couldn't be done in two days or even two months for I had grown up in this type of climate and knew how exhausting it could be. I planned to run this race as slowly as possible because there would be only four days of rest before the Olympic trials.

Sharon and Mom arrived a day before the meet. The next morning, after a late breakfast we drove to New Brunswick. The meet was to take place in the afternoon, the hottest part of the day. The temperature was in the high 80s but the killer was the humidity, which was also at 80 percent. We felt like we were running in a shower. I was already having trouble with my allergies, but fortunately it was still early in the season for the type of pollen that gave me the biggest problem.

This would be the year's first race in which all the top Americans were entered and there would be some collegiate runners as well. Most collegians, in the distances, chose to wait for the Olympic trials. All the strength in events over 1500 meters was in the post-graduate group and in two high school upstarts: Lindgren in the 5000 and Jim Ryun in the 1500.

About 3 p.m. I began to warm up very slowly, doing only

enough to get my body loose so I could move easily. I had to save energy. An hour went by and it was time for the 5000. Included in the field were Lindgren, Beatty, Larrieu, Rodda, Oscar Moore and Bill Dellinger, my chief competitors. All the others were of minor concern. This would be my first race against Dellinger since 1959. I had heard he had accomplished some fine workouts and was tough, but now I, along with many others, wondered just how tough he would be.

We were called to the starting line. Soon the starter raised his pistol and we were off. Lindgren burst out of the pack and soon had the lead. I followed in second with the rest of the field strung out behind. Down the back straight Lindgren pulled away slightly and after the first lap had a seven-yard lead. I made no attempt to catch him and the others were satisfied to stay behind me.

He passed the half-mile in 2:10 and lengthened his lead to 10 yards, but I wasn't concerned with his lead for I knew, if I wanted, I could be in back of him in just a few strides. I wasn't working hard and wanted the pace to be slow so I would be ready for the next weekend.

These old cinder tracks became full of holes as a meet progressed, and this one was bad. Every third or fourth step would land you into one of these holes and your foot would turn slightly. At times it seemed you were spending as much energy trying to run in a straight line as you spent racing. Someday there would be a different surface and the times would come down drastically. But for now we were all in the same situation, no one had an advantage.

Lindgren continued to lead and passed the mile in 4:25 but the positions remained the same behind him. After two more laps, with Lindgren passing the mile and a half in 6:43, Beatty moved out and passed me. Slowly he crept up on Lindgren, but was still behind by six yards at the two mile mark, which Gerry passed in 9:04. I followed Beatty, content to have the pace go so slowly. By 10 laps Beatty had moved to within three yards of Lindgren, while I was still third. Only a few remained in contention as Dellinger and Rodda followed me. Joe Lynch was there, but far back. Larrieu and Julio Marin had dropped out, complaining of the heat.

By the time we came into the straight for the gun lap Beatty had moved directly in back of Lindgren and I was close on Beatty's heels. I was planning my final assault, deciding to wait until we hit the back straight.

The gun sounded and Lindgren picked up the tempo ever so slightly. Beatty was with him but looking tired, and I could sense someone directly in back of me. Around the turn the positions remained the same. I waited and waited, not caring if someone else got the jump on me. I was feeling so good I knew they would need a lot left to beat me.

Finally, with 250 yards to go, I couldn't wait any longer. I took one step to the side and turned on the speed. Within two steps I was by Beatty and within 10 meters I was beside Lindgren. I was almost in full sprint now and it would be a race to the tape. I could sense Lindgren giving chase and had six yards on him as we reached the three-mile point.

The time was 13:32.6. I had the jump on the rest of the field and it would take some good running to catch me. I couldn't hear any footsteps as I turned into the final 80 yards, but you never know what is happening back of you, so I continued to drive as hard as I could.

I hit the tape in 13:56.2 with Lindgren following in 13:58.6. Beatty was third in 14:06, and Dellinger moved in on Beatty for fourth with a 14:10.2 clocking. Lindgren had run a 57.5 last lap and I had run 55.1. Pretty good, I thought, since the sprint didn't come until the last 250 yards. My last 188 yards was 23.6, not bad after three miles in this weather. I was really surprised Beatty and Dellinger hadn't run a faster last lap. My confidence was soaring!

That evening I went over the race, as I always did. I knew if I could run that fast over the last part of the race I could run much faster. Obviously you can't sprint if your legs are tired and I had felt so good going into the last lap. Well, I thought, I could have run ten seconds faster without any trouble. That would be realistic. That would be 13:46. If I take the weather conditions into account, because Tokyo will be cool compared to this, I can take off another second per lap for a 13:34 finish. And the track in Tokyo will be much better than this. What it comes down to is that I can run below the world record right now and I have four more months to train.

The next few days were relaxed with easy running in the morning before the sun was high and in the evening when the shadows were long. I enjoyed training alone these few days. The days went by quickly.

Soon it was the morning of the race and we drove to Randall's Island, New York. The day was hot and thunderstorms were predicted. I hoped a storm came while we were on the track. In this weather I wouldn't mind running in the rain. As the race approached a black cloud appeared and the rains came, for about three minutes. Then it was over and the weather was worse than before. It was so hot and muggy I didn't feel like warming up, but did anyway. Very slowly.

The same people who had been in the AAU meet were entered, plus military champion Billy Mills and the NCAA qualifiers. They included two runners who had tied in winning the NCAA race, Jim Murphy and Bill Straub. Bill had run in the AAU meet.

The hot, humid weather worked against good times, so the pace was slow. It was worse than it had been at the AAU meet. I decided I'd stay well up with the leaders and not allow anyone to break away as I had done with Lindgren in the AAU race.

This Olympic trial was very important because the rules stated that whoever finished first was automatically on the Olympic team as long as he was in shape for the final trial in September. However I wasn't at all convinced they were going to hold to that. I wasn't worried about anybody in particular but I gave consideration to Beatty, Dellinger and Lindgren, as usual. It wasn't too long before the starter fired the gun that sent us on our way for the 5000 final.

As I, and every other knowledgeable track fan expected, Lindgren burst into the lead but this time I went with him. I didn't intend to let him get away. After the first lap I could feel the heaviness of the weather and knew it was going to be a slow and tiring race.

Through three laps Lindgren led, with me in second. On the fourth lap Doug Brown moved to my outside shoulder and then moved in on me. It didn't hurt my strategy, though, and I was content to run third.

Then it seemed everyone wanted to run in second: Dellinger, then Mills moved to the outside and up on my shoulder. There was no alternative but to let the others move in. I found myself back a few more places for no reason at all. I was running in sixth place about halfway through the race. The pace was slow, the mile in 4:30. Four more laps went by and we were coming to the two-mile mark. The time was shouted to us as we passed. "9:12!"

After the two-mile mark I wanted to be close to the front so I moved out and ran past everyone until I was beside Lindgren. My momentum carried me on by and it felt better to be out front where I could use my tactics. Dellinger followed me past Lindgren and Gerry found himself in the same situation I had been in a few laps earlier. Trapped, he was pushed back to ninth.

Soon, however, Lindgren moved to the outside, passed the others and was on my shoulder again, where he ran for awhile. Finally, he again took the lead and I was where I wanted to be. I could move whenever I wanted but I was careful now. I didn't want anyone forcing me back and nobody made an attempt. I am sure they were beginning to feel fatigue.

With three laps remaining Lindgren was leading me with Dellinger close behind. The others had dropped back and were no longer in contention. All I had to do now was decide when to make my final move and hope to catch Gerry and Bill napping. With one and three-fourths laps to go I took the lead and upped the tempo slightly. It wasn't enough to do any damage and I was only feeling myself out to see how much I'd have left for the sprint. I felt good and continued with the pace, trying not to force it any more than I had to.

We were now coming into the gun lap. As we crossed the line the gun fired and I increased the pace slightly. Around the turn and into the back straight. Just as we came off the turn, Dellinger went sprinting by. It was hard to determine if he was all out but I picked up the pace to stay with him with little trouble. We were moving well down the back stretch and I was comfortable, making the decision to stay behind.

We were dropping Gerry now, but he was still in the race with the final straight directly ahead. I moved out and poured everything I had into the final sprint. I was beside Bill in just a few yards and then by him. I was moving away as I broke the finish line.

Bill was back only 10 yards while Gerry finished 25 yards behind. My final time was 14:10.8 with Bill at 14:11.4. Lindgren was third in 14:13.8, while Oscar Moore, Jim Murphy, and Tom

Rodda qualified for the final trials in Los Angeles. Billy Mills had placed eighth and Jim Beatty had dropped out after nine laps.

The time was slow but it didn't matter. I had won under very trying weather conditions. What was so unbelievable was that my allergies were giving me less and less trouble. It seemed the more I ran and the better my conditioning, the healthier I became.

What an incentive. Sharon was happy for me, of course, but Mom was awestruck at the turnabout in my health. I'm sure she wished better health for me my entire life and here she was, an eye witness to it in a way she had never thought possible. That didn't mean I didn't have my troubles. I was probably running at 90 percent in the two races because of my allergies but they were nothing like I had as a teenager.

While my family was happy with my continually improving success, Jim Beatty was having his problems. Jim said he'd petition the Olympic committee to be placed in the final trials because of a calf injury and cut to his foot which had interfered with his training. I agreed with him because he was still considered among the best distance runners in the country and could give strength to the 5000 in Tokyo.

With the Olympics constantly on my mind I drove to our friends apartment that evening thinking of Dellinger, now my main threat for dominance. I sincerely believed no one except Bill would be able to take over the number 1 spot.

With this in mind, there could be no letting down now. I wanted to return to California as soon as possible to get back into training. After a brief stopover in West Milton to visit my father and brothers I left for LA with their well-wishes. The next day Sharon was to drive to the West Coast, stopping to visit her parents in Boise, Idaho. We would meet in LA about two weeks later in time for the USA vs. the USSR meet July 25-26.

My thoughts weren't on the Russians, however, as I trained in the San Fernando Valley, staying at the apartment of my cousin, Ted Metz. I was looking ahead to Tokyo. Everything I did was preparing for that one big race. Anything else I did was only a test to see how I was coming along. With this in mind, I began two full weeks of solid training.

My workouts were the best I had ever done. Day after day I was doing more at faster speeds. Nothing could make me tired and I thought if this continued I would be unbeatable. It was a great feeling.

After Sharon arrived from Idaho we moved to Pomona to temporarily share a rented house with George Young and his wife, Shirley. It would be only until the Russian meet. It was a good arrangement for everyone since we were all good friends and it was economically feasible.

The next week was spent helping the directors of the USA-USSR meet inform the public about the contest. It was arranged that I would be a guest on almost every type of television program in Los Angeles. The easiest of all were the talk shows. That is, all except the one time when I got more than I had bargained for.

I was to appear on a kid's program and thought it should be simple enough. Then, much too late to back out, I discovered that the interviewer was a clown and would be talking to animal puppets during the show. As I waited off camera I became very uncomfortable and quite apprehensive as the clown went through his routine with the puppets. It all seemed so ridiculous. I thought to myself, this might be a very tough show.

During a commercial break the clown came over and introduced himself and the director told us we'd only have a few minutes to promote the USA-USSR meet. We took our places in front of the stage where the puppeteer did his act. As the camera's red light came on, we started to talk.

At first it was all normal conversation until the puppeteer said, "You must feel awful funny running around in your underwear!"

Well, that set off the clown and he started saying some really silly and stupid things to the animal puppets, who laughed like hyenas and bobbed up and down like crazy. I had no idea how to reply. I was the scapegoat of all their jokes. It got more and more ridiculous but there was nothing for me to do except try to remain calm on the outside for my insides were in turmoil. When they asked a silly question, I'd give it a serious answer. It became a game between us and I was definitely out of character. Trying to hold my own, the time seemed endless before the interview was over. I felt like I had run a long, long race where the odds were stacked against me. I was so happy to walk away from that session.

Things began to look up again a few days later when George and I were asked to do an interview between innings of the Dodgers baseball game. This was more like it! We got the royal treatment with the track meet's promotion director chauffeuring us to the stadium and then personally escorting us to the announcer. As we awaited our turn, we listened to an interview with an injured player. When they were off the air, we overheard the director tell the player he'd be receiving an outboard motor worth $500.00, which was in keeping with the interview pay scale. George and I looked at each other and thought this might be a rewarding evening.

Finally it was our turn in front of the microphones. The interview went very well and was quite a step up from the kids' show. Afterward the director said, "We'd like to give both of you a gift for being with us."

"That would be very nice." I said, very excited but trying to keep cool.

"We know you can't accept our normal gift since you are amateurs and therefore we have for both of you a mixer, which I'm sure your wives can use."

We were dumbfounded. George and I looked at each other and said almost in unison, "Being amateurs doesn't matter; we can accept your normal gift."

He just smiled and told us we'd be receiving the gifts in the mail. We didn't want to be greedy, but here we were training much harder than any baseball player had ever trained and we had to abide by the amateur code.

Amateurism -- some day it would be changed, and George and I, along with many others, would be the vanguard of that movement. We wouldn't see the change during our running careers, but those who came after us would benefit. We would just have to keep chipping away at the old rules. We walked away from that interview very angry and looking forward to the day we would have the respect that runners deserved.

Putting this behind us, George and I got our minds back on the race and trained together during the week. He was content to do what I did for most of the workouts but because he was running the steeplechase he spent a part of the workouts in hurdle training off by himself.

It was a good arrangement for us to have each other's company and our days leading up to the meet were very similar in intensity as both of us were to run on the second day of the meet. We worked hard and I felt great until the start of Thursday morning's workout. Something was wrong. I felt stiff and my body seemed tired.

This was not a new experience, it had happened many times before. But to have it happen now, just before the Soviet dual meet, was a catastrophe. I had found my body had fairly regular ups and downs although the reason for them was never explained. I now believe it had something to do with hormone and glandular changes.

This is what would happen: in an up period I would push my body to extreme limits over a period of five to six weeks. At the end of that time, and without warning, I'd go into a tired slump. I couldn't move easily and easy distances of the day before became impossible. After three to five days in this low state I would begin a climb until once again I reached a plateau where my body would respond to anything asked of it. But to have it happen now! In three days I was supposed to step on the track against the Soviets. Feeling like I did, I couldn't possibly run a good race.

That evening after checking into the University of Southern California, where the team was staying, I went to the training room for a rub down, hoping a massage would help those muscles that felt so useless. I went for an easy jog afterward and felt better, though lethargic. I went back to my room and thought about the problem. If this was an out-of-balance hormonal condition, and if the body had to wait for balance to be restored, just maybe I could hurry the process along.

The next morning I drove to Dorsey High School where no one on the team would be around. Of course, Igloi was there.

"Good morning, Coach."

"Morning, Bob, how are you?"

"Not so good. My body is at a low point and I feel very, very tired."

"That is not good," he said. "You run against Russians on Sunday."

"Yes, and if my body doesn't improve, I won't have a chance."

Igloi had seen this happen to the best of his runners over the years, and being a master he could train the body in such a way that he could sometimes put the "slump" off until the big meet was over. However, I wasn't so lucky and I decided to force my body into complete exhaustion to see if it would reverse the cycle in a hurry. I explained to Igloi what I planned and he listened without expression.

"Well, sometimes coach must experiment so I say, good luck."

So, my workout began. I ran repeats at 150 yards as hard as I could go. My body felt as if I was carrying a 50-pound weight on my shoulders and each step was agony. I switched to 220s and then to 100s, gradually bringing my body to near exhaustion. It took only 40 minutes to reach this state. Only a few days before I had done this same workout twice and walked away from the practice track without undue fatigue.

I decided on a last set. Tears came to my eyes as my body rebelled against the hard 150s I was doing. My mind, too, wanted to stop but on I went until my legs were so rubbery, I couldn't take another step. I was exhausted and left the field with Igloi's best wishes. I hoped I had done the right thing. It felt like I might never recover, for I might have pushed my body even further into fatigue. Would my body shut down for an extended time? I didn't know.

During the afternoon I called Dr. Silver and he advised a B12 injection. I was on my way within minutes.

That evening I was too tired to eat much and asked for another massage. I found Stubb Evans and he worked on me for about 40 minutes. I went to bed early, hoping for the best in the morning.

It was Saturday now and I still felt tired, but looser. I jogged, both morning and evening, and spent the day with George Young overlooking the running track where the U. S. and Soviet teams were battling for world superiority.

Neither of us took part in the opening ceremonies but just before the meet we walked to the Olympic Coliseum and found two lounge chairs, which we placed in the shade directly under the Olympic torch, high above the track. From here we had a perfect view and no one would bother us. We spent a pleasant afternoon watching Lindgren beat the Russians at 10,000 meters and observed that the Russians were flat. We'd heard they were doing a lot of sight-seeing and eating plenty of good food and I supposed they were not as sharp as they should have been. We felt we'd have no trouble winning if they didn't run any better than today.

With an easy jog and another early bed time, I awoke feeling better and immediately went to the park to jog. I was still not as sharp as I'd been the week before, not by a long shot, but I knew I'd have no trouble running a respectable race.

I'd met Pytor Bolotnikov the day before at the dining room and he looked confident as we toasted one another with milk for the photographers. He could be very tough since he was the 1960 Olympic champion at 10,000 meters and had a best time of 13:38.1 for the 5,000 meters. He didn't like to lose, either.

My pre-race meal was a late breakfast and afterward I had several hours to waste before walking to the Coliseum. The rest of the time I spent reading a newspaper and doing a dozen other things to keep busy. I finally decided to go over early and watch some of the races.

After dressing for my race it was just a short walk to the Coliseum. As always, I tried to keep calm, not thinking about the race so that I could save the vital adrenaline stored in my body. There were times during race day when I'd find myself thinking over the tactics I might use. Then I'd smile to myself and try to think of something else.

In the days prior to the meets, I always went over in my mind how I would run the race. It was like I was watching a movie of my race. I used this technique for years. But now was not the time; I didn't want to become excited.

This day was not easy for me for I had looked forward to facing the Soviets since 1961 when the Soviet walker twirled his cap in the air and our distance runners were beaten badly. There wasn't any hate, there never had been, but the Soviets were our adversaries, not only in athletics, but in many aspects of our life. It was more than a battle of track powers, it was a battle of ideologies.

I found a folding chair and settled down in almost the same spot as the day before to watch the competition. There was a crowd of some 50,000 witnessing the contest on this bright, sunny day. I reflected on my past, my illness, my injuries, my hard work, my disappointments. I looked up at the beautiful sky. I felt grateful. I looked back at the race that was taking place on the track below.

Event after event went by and the United States was doing well. If this trend continued, we'd beat the Russians handily.

It was time to start my warm-up. I went to a grassy area set aside for the athletes and started my slow jog. Others were going much faster but I was content to allow my body to get used to moving. I saw Dellinger, who was to be my teammate against two Soviets. We stopped and discussed strategy.

"Bill, I think we should let them lead and make our move in the latter stages of the race," I said

"Fine with me," Bill said. "I don't think they have the speed to out-sprint either one of us.

The Soviets still believed the U. S. runners were not strong in the distances. The day before, Soviet coach Gabriel Korobkov had brushed off Lindgren's victory in the 10,000 by saying, "The smog interfered with the breathing of my athletes. The times proved they did not run good race."

It was true. The Soviets had run poorly. Possibly their coach was right. But the Americans had to face the same conditions; most had come from areas other than Los Angeles.

Bill and I decided to follow the Soviets until 300 meters from the finish, when we'd begin our sprint. It was a simple plan. Since Bolotnikov would have to do the leading, it would be his strength against our speed. Both of us thought we could stay with him, no matter how fast he ran.

We continued to jog and loosen up; about 20 minutes before the race, I put on my spikes and did a few sprints. I wasn't sharp, but I felt ready for anything the Soviets tried.

Ten minutes before the race I went inside the Coliseum to be ready for introductions. Bill and the two Soviet competitors were already there and a few minutes later came the announcement introducing us. Together we descended the steps and at the bottom we jogged to the start.

The starter was ready as we slipped out of our warmup clothes and he ordered us to the starting line. We looked at each other for a second, then focused on our race strategies.

"Get set!" The gun fired.

As planned, Bill and I allowed the two Soviets to take the lead and we settled into the third and fourth positions. From the outset it was a slow pace and I smiled to myself that they were playing into our hands. Unlike the United States where the coaches do not tell the runners how to run their races, the Soviets have meetings with their coaches to decide the best tactics. Korobkov had surely laid out the tactics for the 5,000, but I couldn't understand the slow tempo.

While Bill and I followed, Bolotnikov and Orentas traded leads but the pace remained the same. It was a joke. They had to know we had speed. Maybe they were planning a long finish. It was as if they were conceding the race. Many times I thought of taking the lead and upping the tempo, but most importantly, we had to win. We were part of a team. The time wasn't important. I was sure we'd have no trouble winning.

The first mile, then the second, went by. As we came around the far corner, I could see Korobkov yelling to his runners. I wondered what he was telling them.

The next three laps contained no surprises. Bill and I moved in as tightly as possible on their shoulders. We could see the pistol raised in the air for the final lap and as we began it, the gun fired. I wanted to go but I had agreed with Bill that I'd wait until the final 300. Around the turn we went and I could feel the adrenaline flowing. I looked back at Bill just as we went into the back straight as if to say, "Let's go," and then moved to the second lane. Bringing my knees high and dropping my arms into a sprinter position, I flew past the Soviets within a few strides. They had no response. I knew Bill was behind me. I could hear his footsteps.

Down the straight and into the turn, I looked to the inside. Bill was there but the Soviets were already 20 yards behind. I flew into the turn and saw Korobkov sitting on a chair in the infield. I looked at him and couldn't help but smile. We had arrived. The U. S. distance runners would not be the butt of laughter and ridicule from the Soviets or anyone else.

On into the final straight and the tape loomed in front of me. I felt great. My legs were hardly tired as I hit the tape 10 yards in front of Bill, with the Soviets far behind. I had run a 14:12.4 and Bill 14:14.2. My last 440 was in 54.8. Orentas was timed in 14:18 and Bolotnikov in 14:20. From the point of view of crowd appeal, it must have been a boring race. But winning was so important, and that we had done. When I took a victory lap, thousands of people stood and cheered. Maybe it hadn't been so boring for them after all.

The U. S. men won 139-97, and although the women lost 59-48, for the first time the United States trounced the Soviets with a combined score of 187-156. When we went out to celebrate that night, George and I and our wives, along with some close friends, the talk centered on why the Soviets had performed so poorly. Korobkov said they would be ready by Tokyo. We would have to wait and see.

Once again, though, I had to get back to hard training to prepare for the final Olympic trials in September. I refused several offers to compete in Europe for I thought the travel would be too tiring and my training would suffer. My focus was even more intense on Tokyo.

Korobkov had stated the Soviets would peak by the Olympics and would be running much better. I didn't believe in peaks as such. To me, peaks were a state of mind.

Even when a runner becomes physically tired, his body will recover quickly if he lightens his training. But an athlete has to know his body and feel everything that might be going wrong. Staying in a positive state of mind and focusing on a solution were vital to racing well.

A runner's emotional attitude, however, is much harder to control. If he is fed up with training, and the competition is no longer fun, then he'll have a hard time running well. For me? I was having fun. Great fun. I was the best distance runner in the U. S. and one of the best in the world, and I knew that although I was in the best shape of my life, I'd be even better in the months to come.

That is, as long as I continued to train and race sensibly.

TWELVE

Running Faster Than Any Man

The house where we were living with George and Shirley Young was no longer available. We heard that Bob Richards, two-time Olympic champion in the pole vault, had a few apartments east of Los Angeles near the site where all the athletes would assemble after the final Olympic trials.

Bob also owned an old church where he made many of his movies for television. George and I found the church and Bob inside with his cameramen discussing a segment of film regarding the cereal *Wheaties*. We were hoping Bob would give us a break with reasonably priced quarters for the summer. We had a little laugh while we were waiting since we were as poor as church mice, we really should live here.

When Bob finished talking we introduced ourselves and he recognized our names. When we told him our plight he told us that he did have some apartments, but they were in bad shape. That suited us fine as long as they were cheap. We told him we needed them for two months. He said that would work out fine with him since he was trying to sell them anyway.

When I asked him about the rent, he thought a moment and said, "How about $50.00?"

"$50.00!" I exclaimed. "That's great, Bob! $50.00 for two months shows you really care!"

George also replied enthusiastically. Bob gulped as we continued thanking him. I'll never know for sure if he meant $50.00 for the entire two months or what.

But we had a roof over our heads even though the apartments were in terrible condition, as he had said. It was a good thing our wives were as dedicated to seeing this through. We all viewed the Olympics as a worthy goal and no slight inconvenience would stand in our way.

My planning for the next six weeks included two races before the Olympic trials. They would be speed runs because I wanted to concentrate on that aspect of conditioning; endurance would be worked on in training.

The next week went by quickly; the first race was the following Wednesday evening. We drove 40 miles to Pierce Junior College in the San Fernando Valley. After two light days I felt ready for a good race.

The evening was cool and quiet. Many athletes had come to run in the meet. Igloi was there with the Los Angeles Track Club and he was going to run Jim Grelle in the mile with a fast time in mind. Jim was under a schedule that would bring him closer to his goal of making the Olympic team. That gave George and me a great opportunity to run from behind and go for our best times.

An hour later we stepped on the track and the gun sounded. One of Igloi's runners, my ex-roommate Joe Douglas, immediately took the lead and went into a fast tempo for two laps.

On the back straight of the second lap Mike Thornton took the lead and Grelle was running easily in second. I moved into third, trying to stay relaxed. After the 880 Grelle took the lead.

We came through three laps in 3:01.5 and I knew it wasn't as fast as Igloi had wanted. Grelle picked up the tempo and I stayed with him down the back straight. He led around the turn but I could see he was tiring. I moved to his outside shoulder and crept up on him.

With 50 yards remaining, I was ahead by a scant yard and it stayed that way as we went through the tape. My time was 3:58.9. Jim was one-tenth of a second back in 3:59 and very disheartened about his time, even though it was his second-best time of the year. Even with Jim leading for two laps, I had been fortunate to beat him. George ran a life-time best of 4:02.7. All in all, we were quite happy with the day.

A week from Saturday I wanted to run a training race of 1,320 yards or three laps. I wouldn't rest for it, but would see how mentally strong I was by running tired.

George and I continued to train together at the LaVerne College football field, our early morning sessions at 6 a.m. It was a grass workout based on the Igloi system. I was doing one hour and fifteen minutes of speed work, repeat 100 and 150 yards, totaling about seven miles. All rest intervals had been shortened so I wouldn't have much rest. As I went about my training, George did his own training in the area. In the afternoon we went to Pomona College where there was a large grass field more suitable for longer intervals. Both of us were taxing our systems more and more. All our training that week culminated at the Mt. San Antonio track for the three-quarters time trial to see where we were in our training.

Because this was not a race we had gone along with the plan not to rest. Both of us felt heavy but strong. Our trial was successful. I ran 2:56.8 and George 2:59.8. Our training was going as planned.

The following Saturday we were to race at Pierce one last time and I thought about the race I would run. I didn't need another mile and I didn't want to run a 5000 either, so it seemed like the two-mile would be a good choice. For several days I thought about the best course to follow and talked it over with George. Then after much more thought, knowing I could run a fast time over the distance, I decided to try to break the world record at that distance. The record holder was Michael Jazy, at 8:29.6, who would be my best competition in the games. My breaking his record would really give him something to think about.

George and I discussed strategy in the livingroom of our apartment.

"George, I really think I can go through the first mile in 4:12."

"That's too fast for me Bob. I think it'd be better to run 4:14; I feel I can run that and keep going for awhile."

I looked at him and thought about how this might sound to an outsider. It would be like a team assessing the difficulties of climbing Mt. Everest. I thought for a second, "Well, if we can keep the pace even we can still break the record. Okay, 4:14 it is."

George sat there exuding the confidence he always seemed to have. Then he said, "I'll lead as long as I can but when I get tired you'll be on your own." It was almost as if Igloi were here giving us the race plan.

It wasn't ego talking like this but confidence in our abilities backed by the training and the world-class times we were both running. American distance running was becoming a powerful force and George and I both knew we were leaders in that drive. We wanted to bring the two-mile record back to the United States.

Even though we were going to make an assault on the record, we didn't curtail our regular training and worked hard those two weeks, looking ahead to the Olympic games rather than the two-mile race. I was doing a lot of experimenting with my workouts and also with my shoes. I had been on the free list with Adidas for some time and they sent me shoes from Germany. I had just received a new royal blue model that fit perfectly. As I started running, however, something did not seem right. A few strides later I realized it was not the shoe but the color. My vision was such that I could see the shoes every time I took a step and knew I could not wear them in the upcoming races. The color was just too distracting.

I called the Adidas representative, Dick Banks, about my problem and he had Germany air-mail another pair within the week This time they were tan. This was also a new model, and of all things, it was called the *Tokyo*! They fit perfectly and the color didn't bother me.

The problem with all racing shoes up to that time was the fact they didn't have a heel. I always had an Achilles problem and the lack of a heel stretched the tendon every time I took a step. I took the shoes to a local shoemaker, and after telling him what I wanted, he looked through his supplies until he found a heel that fit the shoe well enough to do the job. He glued it on and I had the world's first pair of track spikes with heels. (I wish I had patented the idea.) The next day, during my workout, I found they did the job beautifully and decided they'd be my racing shoes from now on.

I continued my training, thinking of the Olympics until Aug. 29. It was now time to try to run faster than any man had ever run in the two-mile.

George and I, along with our families, once again drove to

Pierce Junior College, arriving about 6:30 on a cool, pleasant evening. Although there were only about 300 people in the stands, they were enthusiastic and track-wise. Still I was concerned over the lack of excitement for big competition and thought it might be impossible to get "up" for the race.

I visualized the mile race some two weeks earlier and remembered how the track had been full of holes when we finally raced. The dirt track was alright for a while but after several races there would be small divots made by the spikes as the runners pushed off. That made it so hard to run on dirt or cinder tracks for the holes made your ankles turn when you hit one and that happened constantly. They also didn't rebound. On the tentative program the two-mile was scheduled for late in the evening, and by then the track would be a mess.

George and I approached Pete Peterson, who was in charge of the meet, and told him of our plan. Because there was no printed program for this certified AAU meet, and there was such a loose schedule of events, they could be changed. Pete agreed to move the two-mile up to the second event. With this done we relaxed on the grass until it was time to warm up. My body felt good as I thought about the test to come.

An effective technique I had used for several years was again about to prove its worth. As I lay there I ran the race in my mind. I could see myself in the race situation. It was almost as if I was remembering a race that had already been run. In this instance I pictured myself relaxing behind George for the first mile or more. I could see myself going around the track, running smoothly and effortlessly. I could even see myself becoming tired but concentrating on the tempo. Then there was the final drive, not allowing my body to falter even though I was tired. I felt confident as I again opened my eyes. In today's terminology, this strategy is called "positive imaging or visualization." Fancy words for a technique I had used for years. All I knew then was that it worked.

The temperature was just right and the air was clear in the San Fernando Valley. We were up wind from any possible smog and I knew my allergies wouldn't give me trouble. Also, with hard training with little rest, I was strong and knew my strength would carry me through.

As the schedule was announced over the loudspeaker we had an hour to go. George and I began our slow warm-up as did the other runners. Some of the Igloi runners and Billy Mills were going to run. As the race neared, I slipped on my spikes for a few sprints.

The announcement came for us to report and we made our way to the start. Pete Peterson announced the race participants and as he came to me he said, "And in lane two, Bob Schul, who is going to break the world record tonight at two miles!"

I looked at him in disbelief, what a shock! I hadn't expected him to announce this! The adrenaline poured through me now. It was working to my advantage. All of a sudden we weren't playing around. I could feel the excitement of the crowd wondering if this were some kind of joke. The pressure was on. I've got to do it!

The starter called us to the line. George was to my inside with Mills on my right shoulder. It was a big field of 14 athletes and I hoped they wouldn't interfere. As we waited those few seconds for the gun, my mind focused on the race. I thought of nothing else. The crowd disappeared from my senses and I concentrated on what I must do.

The gun sounded and George leaped into the lead, hitting the required tempo in just a few strides. Around the turn and into the back stretch he smoothed out, running relaxed. I settled in behind him with the others stretched out behind.

Around the far turn and into the straight toward the end of the first lap, the official yelled as we passed, "Sixty-one!"

I thanked George in my mind for doing the job perfectly. As we continued around the turn the pace was perfect. In the middle of the back stretch, Norm Higgins went around me and took the lead from George. I couldn't believe it! The pace hadn't slowed and we were on world record time. What was he trying to do?

Norm held the pace and we came into the half-mile in 2:05, just where we had wanted to be. As we swept into the turn, Mills went by and assumed the lead from Higgins. Norm held on for 30 yards and then fell back. George moved out and around and I followed on his shoulder. Within a few steps we were on Billy's shoulder and were running smoothly again.

Down the back stretch I thought Mills was slowing, but I wasn't sure. I didn't want to go too fast either. Coming out of the turn, however, I knew Mills had slowed the tempo, and I shouted, "Billy, faster! "

Instantly Mills quickened his stride. George and I followed. As we came to the end of the third lap Billy slowed again and this time George moved out, ready to pass. By the time we went by the three-quarter mile mark, we had both passed Billy.

"3:10" was the time yelled to us as we went by, still on pace. I felt great at this point. If only George could keep it up. We had outrun our competitors now and George could concentrate on pace. I could concentrate on his shoulder.

Mills was back five yards as we went down the back stretch of the fourth lap and I was so close to George one mishap would have meant the end for both of us. I couldn't hear anything except the sound of our spikes hitting the track.

Around the turn and into the end of the first mile we went. I could see George was tiring but he wasn't slowing. We hit 4:14 perfectly, although it had been a bit erratic getting there. George had picked up the pace on the fourth lap and he was holding it. If we were to break the record, we'd have to keep up this pace.

The jockeying during the second and third laps had been taxing and now the question was, could we keep going? George wasn't wavering and we continued the fast pace around the turn and into the back stretch. It was just the two of us against the clock now, everybody else was far behind. Thoughts were pouring through my mind as I concentrated on George's shoulders. He was tiring, I could see that. But he must continue. He must!

We came into the end of the fifth lap and for the first time I could hear the crowd. They were screaming as they sensed the world record was in sight. I shut them out again, as I put all my concentration on the race.

"5:17" was shouted. I felt good that we had continued the fast pace. Three laps left and in my mind I pleaded with George to keep going.

Around the turn and into the back straight and his shoulders were showing tightness. I knew he couldn't last much longer and I had to be careful he didn't slow down. But there was no slowing as George continued. Around the turn and toward the end of the sixth lap, George was giving it all he had but he was weakening fast.

For the first time I felt my body starting to fade. As we approached the timer George moved into the second lane and I knew it would now be up to me. As I passed George, the timer called, "6:22" and I knew I'd have to quicken the pace if the record were to be broken.

I was tiring fast and had no idea if I could do it. I tried to pick up the pace as I moved down the back stretch but I wasn't sure if I did. With 660 to go my body was rebelling. I berated myself for not resting prior to the race. I wasn't even sure if I could finish.

I could see my fellow athletes yelling to me but my mind wouldn't register the words. I felt their confidence. It didn't matter. They gave me what I needed.

My muscles were working as fast as they could now and I knew there would be no last-minute sprint. It would have to be a long even finish and with 550 yards to go I put everything I had into it. I heard "7:25" when I passed the timer, then the gun sounded.

All right, I thought. The record is yours if you've got the guts to run for it. Run! Now! My legs were aching with fatigue and my mind was bursting but there were only 440 yards to go. Do it!

Down the back stretch the other athletes had lined up along the track and were shouting at me. I tried to increase the tempo. It was useless, my legs were dead, there was no spring left.

Into the final turn I concentrated on lifting my knees. Drive, damn you, drive! One-hundred fifty yards to go, a lousy 150 yards! Lift ... Drive ... Lift ... Drive! I could see the tape across the track now.

Closer it came. My body was one mass of hurt. I cursed myself again. Fifty yards to go ... 40 ... 30 ... 20 ... Three more steps and into the tape. Thank, God! It's over! My body relaxed as the pain subsided. The crowd was going wild. Had I done it? Was I now a world record holder? An official ran to me.

"You've broken the record!" he shouted.

I did it. Yes! I did it! I was so happy. It had been worth it. Every last step. All that agony and pain and training and, oh, I didn't care. That's what it was all about. Who could take the most. It had all been put together by teamwork and most of all by my gutsy friend George Young.

The final time was announced as I cooled down in the infield.

My head was aching as I listened for the official watches to be read. They announced I had set a new record in 8:26.4, breaking the old mark by 3.2 seconds. Mills was second in 8:45.6, more than 150 yards behind.

If the Europeans hadn't believed I'd be a threat in the games, they'd have to now. If I could continue to build, I felt I had a real chance to win the 5,000 meter gold medal in Tokyo.

THIRTEEN

Final Olympic Trials

It was Aug. 29 and I had two weeks before the final U. S. Olympic trials. I trained hard until three days before the race then switched to very easy workouts. I felt as ready as I ever would be.

This would actually be an easier race than the first trials because some of the runners wouldn't be competing in the 5,000 but only in the 10,000. Only the top six from the first trials were eligible plus Jim Beatty, who had successfully petitioned the Olympic committee to compete.

Besides Beatty there were Tom Rodda, Jim Murphy, Oscar Moore, Gerry Lindgren, and Bill Dellinger, the only threat to me. If a person could be confident of making the Olympic team, I was that person. The race was almost anticlimactic. I wanted to run close to 13:43 because I thought that's what it would take to qualify in the heats in Tokyo.

Since the race was on a Sunday I'd take it easy on Monday and then do a test workout Tuesday evening. I'd see then if I was ready for the two races, the October 16th trials and the October 18th final. The only other concern I had now was injury. It was the first time I'd gone without a major injury since the beginning of my international running. I couldn't slack off on my training. I just had to be very careful.

On Saturday, the first day of the competition, Lindgren won the

10,000 defeating Mills and Larrieu but in the process he raised a blister on one of his toes and decided to drop out of the 5,000. That dropped the field to six. It was a good thing the Olympic committee had seen fit to allow Beatty in the race or we could have drawn straws for the medals.

The next day it was my turn to go to the starting line. The September weather was bright and beautiful. There was no smog and my allergies wouldn't be affected. However, no matter how much confidence I had, I always worried about everybody in the race the hour before. In the warm-up area everybody looked good, and it was never certain when someone would run a spectacular race.

Dellinger was there and we talked awhile before continuing our jogging. He had read that I wanted to run 13:43 and he realized, as well as I, that the field would be scattered if it were that fast. I told him I wasn't against coming in together because I didn't want to go into an all-out sprint and take the chance of an injury. He agreed that the games were more important than winning this race so we decided if we were together with 330 yards left we wouldn't sprint. Up to that point we'd be on our own.

It came time to walk to the Coliseum for the race and I walked down the steps to the spot where the 5,000 would start. The others were milling around looking anxious, especially Beatty, who was as nervous as a cat. I guess he had every right to be because things had gone so badly for him all year. Dellinger was the only one who seemed calm.

Soon the starter called us onto the track and the public address announcer introduced us. Here we were, six athletes vying for three team spots, each with his own thoughts. We were lined up now waiting for the gun. It sounded and we were off.

I immediately assumed the lead and continued to hold for one and a quarter miles. There was little excitement as the others were content to follow. The first mile was slow, about 4:30, and I realized I wouldn't run 13:43. I wanted the pace to be even, just as it would be in the Tokyo trials, so I didn't pick it up.

After five laps Oscar Moore took the lead and led through two and one half miles. We had reached the two-mile mark in 9:05 and it felt as though I were on a nice jog. The pace was getting even slower so I again assumed the lead with Dellinger a stride back.

Moore dropped back into fourth behind Murphy, who was five yards back of Dellinger. Both Beatty and Rodda had started falling back after two miles and were now more than 80 yards behind.

I increased the pace enough to pull away from Murphy, who immediately started falling back. It was all over now. There was no threat of my not making the Olympic team.

Moore had re-passed Murphy and had 20 yards on him as we went into the final lap. Around the turn I went and into the back straight. Suddenly Bill Dellinger was on my shoulder and surprised me by pulling a step in front. My reflexes immediately reacted and I pulled even again. I looked at him and then glanced behind.

"He's pretty far back, " I said. He glanced around to take a look. "We'll go in together," he said.

It was agreed. We'd keep the same pace and go in side by side. Around the last turn, Bill was on my outside shoulder. Then, from out of the stadium came an unfamiliar sound. I could hear people booing. There weren't many but it hit me hard.

Didn't they understand the significance of this? We were the first two American distance runners in Olympic history who were finally given a chance of winning the gold medal! Not a shot in the dark but true contenders for the honor. It wasn't that we would be lucky and win but that someone else might be lucky and beat us. I had to tune these people out but it was difficult to do.

We hit the tape together, glancing back to see how Moore was doing. After two deep breaths we were completely recovered. We had run 13:55.6. Oscar was third in 13:58.8, a personal best. Murphy was fourth in 14:04.6. Beatty was fifth in 14:21.6 and Rodda sixth in 14:28.2. I was surprised Beatty hadn't placed third. With his experience and another month of training, we could have had three athletes with the potential to win three medals. It didn't seem fair that such a great runner wouldn't be on the team. It was too bad to end his career like this after he had been among the world's best in '61, '62, and '63.

Later that day I watched the 1,500 meters, a tremendous race. After a fast first lap and slow second lap, Tom O'Hara took the lead and picked up the tempo considerably. With a lap to go six runners were together, and I was yelling my head off for my friend Jim Grelle. He was tucked in behind O'Hara, in a position where he could get boxed. It all opened up on the back stretch with Grelle challenging O'Hara.

Around the turn Grelle was on O'Hara's shoulder and as they moved into the final 100 yards, Burleson burst through and opened a lead. He moved away as O'Hara and Grelle had wasted themselves trying to battle one another on the turn.

It was obvious that Burleson would win with O'Hara almost a sure bet for second. But in third Jim Ryun was moving in on Grelle, who was still ahead with 10 yards to go. All of a sudden Grelle stumbled and started to fall. It was then that Ryun moved ahead and placed third. It wasn't fair. Grelle had beaten Ryun in every race during the year and in this one meet lost by so narrow a margin.

I had trouble holding back the tears as Jim lay on the track just past the finish line. There wouldn't be any ruling to place Grelle on the team in front of Ryun, for all the officials wanted Ryun to make the team. It would give him valuable experience, they said. Baloney! He wasn't ready for international competition. Grelle had a chance to win the gold; Ryun had none.

If there was ever a time when a committee should use its good judgment for the strength of the team, it was in this instance. The team could take Ryun along for the trip but let the runner with the skill and experience battle those with similar experience. Jim Grelle was that runner.

Anybody could see that Ryun would be a great runner in a short time, but the experience he'd gain in one or two races in Japan wouldn't help him to any significant degree. It wasn't a question of allowing a young kid to get the experience or to allow an old veteran to bow out gracefully. It was a matter of selecting the best for the team and Grelle had proven himself all year long.

Feel as I may about the inequities of the system, I knew nothing would change the rules concerning Grelle and Ryun and I had to accept it. Letting the disappointment of my friend's last chance for the Olympics go, I had to get on with my own training.

All the qualifiers moved into the training camp located in a retreat just outside Pomona. Our apartment was only a few miles from the camp. George and I had talked with the team manager and the other officials and received permission to stay with our families and to continue training by ourselves. The team was going to train at the sites where we trained in the evenings: Cal Poly and Mt. SAC, only three miles apart. They were even going to give us a per diem, which was against the rules, but for the first time they were being sensible.

A day passed and we were now in our "test" day. After loosening up in the morning we were prepared to test ourselves at the Cal Poly track that afternoon. Most of the distance runners were going to train there while the rest of the athletes would go to Mt. SAC. Among others, Dellinger and Ryun were there and they decided to join us in our type of workout. Payton Jordan, one of the assistant coaches, agreed to time us.

The workout was simple but it was the best way I had found to determine one's conditioning. It was a series of quarter miles, the first three run in the same time and every fourth one two to three seconds faster. I was running the three in 60 seconds with each fourth in 58. I had always stopped at 20 quarters although there were times I could have gone on. I was sure of this because I always ran the 20th 440 "all out" between 54 and 55 seconds.

If I could run that fast then it should have been possible to string together another four or five at a 60-second pace. My interval had come down to 140 yards with the first 70 walking and the remainder in a slow jog back to the starting line.

This was my favorite test workout and I had done it many times in the past months. I had always done the "test" after doing two to three days of easy training but now I would see how far I could go with my body somewhat fatigued from Sunday's race.

After warming up we were ready. We'd run in single file with each runner taking his turn leading. I was to run first and I finished the quarter in 60 seconds, just what we wanted. George and Bill did likewise on the second and third quarters and then it was Ryun's turn to lead the fast 440.

As we jogged toward the starting line, I could see Jim was nervous. Making the team had seemed to overwhelm him and we were all trying to help his self-confidence. He turned to me as if to say "you take it," but I told him to go. He shot forward like a scared rabbit. As we flew around the turn and down the back straight it was all I could do to stay with him. He was going much faster than we wanted but never would I allow him to pull away.

As we finished he placed his hands on his knees in fatigue while the rest of us turned to take our 140-yard interval. I looked at Payton as he said, "54.1." It was a fast quarter. Now it was going to be tough because moving that fast builds up a lot of lactic acid in the muscle tissue. George told Jim to catch up with us on the interval for we still wanted to make them as even as possible.

It was my turn to lead, and after the 140 jog we moved out at a more relaxed pace. We hit 61 seconds but much more effort had to be put into it. We continued switching the lead and at the end of eight quarters Jim wanted to drop out but we encouraged him to keep going.

At 10 quarters he said he was going to quit, but he lasted through 12, when George and Bill also finished. When Bill dropped out at 12, it gave me a lot of confidence where he was concerned. I knew he would still be tough, but I didn't think he could beat me. I felt so good I ran four more by myself. After finishing the last four, I still felt fine. My legs were tired, but very strong and the test had been a success.

It proved to me that I was ready for whatever happened in the race. Payton gave me a sheet of paper with the lap times: 60, 61, 62, 54.5, 61, 60, 61, 58.5, 62, 59.5, 60, 59.5, 60, 60.5, 61.5 and 56.5. They could run the race any way they wanted: fast, slow, or by switching the tempo (as the Olympic champion Vladimir Kuts of the USSR had done in Melbourne in 1956.) It would make no difference.

We had two weeks more of training before leaving for Tokyo and it would be more than a month before I was to race again. I was concerned about this because racing keeps a runner sharp. All I could do, though, was to continue my training and try to increase the intensity of my workouts so no one else in the world would be able to do them. I knew all the world's distance runners were trying to do the same thing, of course, but who would be the most successful would be answered in the Olympic stadium.

No matter how ready I was, even with a high dose of positive thinking, I knew an athlete could never let down in his constant assessment of himself. If he became confident to the point of complacency he would never become a champion. There would always be one more athlete who would beat him. Instead, you take the hard training, positive thoughts, and re-evaluation of self to build on what you already know yourself to be. In my case I knew I was the BEST distance runner, ever, in the United States. And I was going to prove I was the best 5,000-meter runner in the world.

After the assessment the work was even harder to become better. I therefore thought about several specific things during my workouts. The first was the natural reflexes, which although hereditary, can be sharpened. I went about honing my reflexes to a razor's edge.

Secondly, an athlete's body build was a factor in the type of workouts he attempted, and because I was small-boned and easily injured, I couldn't pound out the long distances that a larger-boned runner like the great Australian, Ron Clarke, could do.

While I had a long history of injury, Clarke was virtually injury free. I always chose grass areas where the pounding on my body structure would be less. But the most important ingredient a distance runner must have is the mental attitude that will allow him to spend the long, necessary hours on the training fields and to train his mind to push his body beyond what another athlete will do.

There is a big difference in the pain levels among athletes and while some are able to continue driving even when their bodies are hurting, others will succumb to the pain and slow down. In my training I brought my body to the pain threshold and forced it through time after time. In the process I conditioned my mind to handle more and more pain.

I was constantly achieving new plateaus in my training by setting up new workouts that were faster and longer. I was spending less time on the rest intervals. It was still the same Igloi theory of training. That never changed. New plateaus could be attempted only after the body had become used to the one it was on and I had to be careful not to attempt workouts when my body wasn't ready for them else I became injured. However, if I waited too long to progress to the next level, I would fail to place enough stress on my body to improve all the vital areas at the maximum rate. In those last weeks I thought how nice it would have been to have Igloi worrying about my training.

After the test workout George and I didn't see much of the team because they worked out in the early afternoon. We found it better to wait until 5:30 p.m. By that time the winds had driven the smog from the field, making it very pleasant. Only Russ Hodge, who had made the team in the decathlon, was training with us in the morning as I continued to give him his running schedule.

I had gone on to one of my new plateaus after the final trials and my morning workouts were long, hard and fast. They were much harder than when I had been with Igloi; I had doubled the distance and increased the speed while cutting down the rest interval. The afternoons had improved also and my goal by the day of the games was to be able to run below 13:30 and at the same time have my 440 time down to 48 seconds.

My plan was to train hard until the day we left for Tokyo, arriving there 18 days before my trial race. I then wanted to taper my training for a few days so I could acclimate, then get in some good workouts up until a week before the trial race on October 16th. If I could continue this progress I would go into the race so full of confidence that I would be ready no matter how the race was run.

Everything was going well for me. I felt very lucky that the time of the games, as well as the site, was in the best setting possible for me. I knew if the games had been held in Europe in the summer, I would not have been able to compete because my allergies would not have allowed me to breathe efficiently. In Tokyo the games were to start after the monsoon season which meant the air would be clean of all pollen. It would be even better than in California.

Before leaving for Japan we had to have various shots to protect us but the Olympic committee had yet to schedule them. In fact, they probably would wait until the final days before leaving. I didn't want to wait until the last minute in case there might be a reaction so I called my friend Dr. Harry Silver. He thought it was a good idea to have the shots early, as had several of the Striders. He offered to give Sharon and me the shots and we started the series of inoculations that day. By the end of the week we were finished. We had no reactions and no loss of training time. All was well.

About a week before we were to leave George and I were training at Cal Poly when a small group of other distance runners came to the field. Among them was Jim Ryun and we asked him if he wanted to join us. He agreed and after we finished jogging put on our spikes and began. We were running repeats of 330s, 220s and

150s at different speeds and an hour went by with all of us still together.

We had just finished a set and were going back to 330s when Jim told us his back hurt. Because we weren't going to run hard we talked him into doing just a few. After two he told us his knee was hurting and it was then George and I looked at each other and understood.

He still was overwhelmed with the whole idea of the Olympics and he wanted to quit from being tired more so than from injury. Not only was he tired from the workouts but from the mental strain as well. He was still in high school and he felt the pressure. Possibly George and I had learned to live with it. We talked Jim into doing one more but we couldn't budge him after that.

George and I went on for another 45 minutes, after which he did some hurdle work on the track while I did some hard 150s with a 20-yard interval.

During our cooling down period Jim joined us again and George told him he mustn't ever give in to himself on the practice field. If he did, he'd do the same thing in races. It was a valuable lesson for this rookie, something he would possibly remember as he drove himself to become the great champion he was destined to be, winning the 1,500 silver medal in Mexico City just four years later.

The last week went quickly. We were outfitted with the official clothes and other items all Olympic teams were given. We were all ready now except for a few athletes who still had to have their last shots. Bob Hayes, tabbed by the media as the "world's fastest human," needed his. I was in the room where the uniforms were being distributed when the team doctor came in and began to prepare the syringe.

All of a sudden there was a yell and Bob went flying to the other end of the room. The doctor stood there with the syringe in his hand. He hadn't even touched Bob. I have never seen anyone so frightened of receiving an injection and for the next few minutes team members roared as the doctor tried to entice Bob back to the table. It took a lot of persuading but finally he ambled back, and with his eyes tightly shut, he received the serum from the waiting syringe. We patted him on the back for bravery as he shuffled away, shaken.

We packed and moved out of our apartments the next day. We were to leave that evening. Sharon and Shirley Young were going on a charter flight arranged by the AAU the next week. Sharon was the recipient of a generous gift from my hometown, West Milton. The entire town of 3,500 had a hand in sending her $800.00 for air fare and accommodations while she was in Tokyo.

School children had rung every doorbell in the community for donations while other people who had been following my progress also contributed. With that check came a telegram with the names of all those generous people. The names included the doctor who had saved my life as a baby, men who had employed me while I was in high school and in college, my coaches, teachers, and many good friends. I had a deep sense of gratitude as I read their message:

Dear Bob:

This is our way of expressing to you the pride we feel in our hearts at this time. The entire community has gained in civic pride from your achievements and representation. When you face the starting line and look up at the throng in that vast stadium, you'll not be alone; for sitting there in spirit, and cheering you on, will be 3500 happy and emotion-packed citizens of West Milton. As the race is in progress, there will be 3500 heartbeats running in unison to yours. When you start your kick in that last lap, there'll be 3500 people praying for you to have the strength to do your best. Win ... lose ... or draw, you're a champion and first-class citizen in the minds and hearts of the people of this community. Good luck and God bless you!

Sharon and I were deeply moved to receive such sentiments. We were indeed two fortunate people.

On September 27th, just one day before my 27th birthday, we boarded the large jet airliner that would take us to Tokyo and the greatest race of my life. I had dreamed about this moment for a long time, a very long time indeed. I settled back in my seat and relaxed as the aircraft lifted off the Los Angeles runway. Soon we were cruising at an altitude of 40,000 feet, going to Alaska where we would refuel before flying over the North Pole to Tokyo!

FOURTEEN

Tokyo

It wasn't long before we landed in Alaska and 14 hours later we arrived in Tokyo. As we left the aircraft we were met by Japanese officials who ushered us into a nearby hangar. Our shot records were checked while luggage was brought to us. We then boarded buses as our luggage was placed on trucks to follow us to the Olympic Village.

A pretty Japanese girl went along as our hostess and answered questions concerning the city. We traveled over new roads built especially for the games. The largest city in Japan was an imposing sight with banners flying everywhere. Everything seemed ready for this sports spectacular.

We arrived at the Olympic Village within 45 minutes and were issued temporary passes before entering the compound. The Village was set up in a former U. S. Army base and looked very much like Oxnard, where I had been stationed.

We reached the building where we were to stay and could see the Soviet flag flying next door. This was the men's part of the village. After we had piled out of the bus and collected our baggage off the trucks, one of the officials gave us our housing instructions. There would be three of us to a room in most instances. Then he started to read off the names for the first room assignments,

"Jay Luck, Rex Cawley. . .

A big yell went up from the assembled athletes. Both Jay and Rex were hollering. They wouldn't room with each other, a typical reaction for athletes in the same event.

The flustered official didn't know what to do. A chorus of voices said they wanted to choose their own roommates. He could do nothing but say, "Alright, you can have any of the rooms on the second and third floors."

George and I went to the top, the least accessible room in the building, where we'd be away from the noise. We arranged our gear and went to find out where we'd be eating and training.

We acquired our meal tickets and made our way to the cafeteria which we had passed on our way in. On this side of the village there were five eating places and because the U. S. team was so large we were assigned one of the halls all to ourselves.

The food was very good and we could eat as much as we wanted of chicken, steak, pasta, rice, fish, potatoes, and all kinds of fresh vegetables. Milk and ice cream were always available as were various soft drinks.

As always, I skipped the soft drinks but ate everything else. I ate the red meat sparingly. The food satisfied me so much I had to be careful not to eat to excess.

I slept well that night and awoke the next morning fully refreshed. Although a track had been built in the village the area was too crowded for me because I didn't like running with people around all the time. And besides, I wanted to keep my training secret.

George and I decided to find another place for our training and that afternoon we boarded one of the shuttle buses that traveled around the different venues of the games. These buses were for the competitors and Olympic staff only. Riding around Tokyo we finally spotted a 400-meter track laid out on a grassy area and left the bus to check it out. We decided the area was perfect for us.

As we warmed up it seemed the grass was uneven and with further checking found it was new sod, probably laid within the last few weeks. However, it was getting late and I decided to use the area for that day only. It proved to be a mistake for it was just bumpy enough that my foot turned slightly each time it landed.

Two days later, although I had switched areas, both Achilles became so swollen and painful that I could hardly jog. I went to the training room for treatment. I had been stupid to train on the uneven area.

At the training room I was told that the special equipment that could help me had not yet arrived from California. The trainers were as upset with the officials in charge of transportation as I was. I had to do something, though, and thought about one of the Japanese hospitals.

Luckily, a Japanese hospital was located in the village just 100 yards from our quarters. They gave me ultrasonic treatments twice a day for four days,. Finally the pain left. Only then was I able to resume full workouts. My training had been curtailed to light jogs during this time and I hoped I hadn't lost any sharpness.

On the second day in Tokyo I found a small 300-meter track situated 200 yards from the main stadium and used it throughout the games. This track was situated next to the gymnastic building and every day after my evening workout I'd watch the Russian gymnasts train. I don't know what they thought as I observed them, sitting there in my USA sweats, but there were some funny looks that first day.

By this time Sharon and Shirley had arrived by charter. Shirley was staying with most of the other wives in a downtown hotel but Sharon was staying with her brother's friends, who lived in Yokohama. We didn't have the money for her to stay in a hotel.

With the intensity of my training schedule and the distance between Tokyo and Yokohama there was little time for us to spend together, except when I rode with her on the train to the friends' home after she had spent the day sightseeing with Shirley and the other wives.

Even that had to stop because it was so late when I got back to the village. I viewed the entire Olympic scene as business, a business I had desperately worked for. This was no time to be letting down the preparation I hoped would culminate in the greatest moment in my life -- winning the gold medal.

We had been in Tokyo almost a week now and the routine was the same every day. George, Russ Hodge, and I would train together in the morning. I continued to give Russ his morning schedule. In the afternoon he and George trained at other places.

George had to have hurdles to jump and Russ was working on his field events.

Our transportation was interesting. George and I would awaken at 6 a.m. and meet Russ at 6:15. Then we'd look for bicycles to ride to the front gate where we would catch a bus to the small track. It was only 300 meters but it became a game in the morning to find the bicycles that were throughout the village. The Japanese had more than 500 of them on the ground, available to all.

Each morning they'd be hidden in bushes and other secret places, waiting on the athlete who had placed them in hiding the night before. We were among the few who arose so early that there were always a few within reach.

The bikes didn't last long, however, as the rate of breakdowns was very high. On one occasion we witnessed a comical sight involving just such a "breakdown!"

A Russian weight lifter, who weighed close to 300 pounds, attempted to ride a bike. To top it off he placed his friend on his shoulders. Almost immediately the bike broke in two pieces with this huge man and his friend tangled among the works. Fortunately no one was hurt, but this was one bicycle that would not be ridden again during the Olympiad.

Another minor incident occurred which, although not comical, allowed me to enjoy a more casual atmosphere with the Japanese. One evening after my workout I ate fish for dinner. I had trouble breathing and broke out in hives. I had stupidly eaten a food that occasionally gave me an allergic reaction. It was imperative to remember every minute detail to keep my body in perfect condition but every so often I made a mistake.

When I arrived at the doctor's room for an injection to counteract the reaction, I found the door locked and a note saying he'd be gone for a few hours. I hurried across the street to the Japanese hospital and explained my problem. I was ushered into a room for an injection. The doctor was also going to give me pills so I waited for him in the lobby.

The lobby was full of Japanese nurses and technicians watching a preliminary game of the womens' volleyball tournament. The doctor was having trouble finding the right medication so I watched the game with the Japanese. The score was very close and each time the other team made a point there were loud groans from the assembly. When the Japanese made a point there were reserved cheers.

The doctor kept running back and forth to see the game each time he heard the excitement until I finally persuaded him to watch the rest of the game before getting my medicine. Because the injection was doing its job he happily agreed. When the Japanese finally won, a happier and prouder people would have been hard to find at that moment.

The days went by and I was feeling perfect again. It had been raining more than usual for this time of year and we were told the monsoon season had been late in arriving. We were witnessing the tail end of it. It seemed to rain every other day; when it did the days were dark and cold. We all were hoping it would end before the track and field events started.

During these days of waiting a great amount of "psyching" was going on and one day I was on the receiving end. It was during a noon meal and I was going through the cafeteria line. One of our officials ran up to me very excited.

"Have you heard the news?" he asked.

I looked at him amazed. "What news?" Was something wrong back home?

He told me he had just heard from a very reliable source in New York that Michel Jazy had broken the world record for 5000 meters in a workout just prior to coming to Tokyo. I thanked him for that valuable piece of information but was skeptical of it. If, indeed, he had broken the record, he'd be my main opposition.

Finally, on October 10th, the games opened and the day was beautiful. We were assembled outside the Olympic stadium with the other athletes from around the world. Music played and finally the announcement of the United States of America was made. It was a thrill to march into the Olympic stadium to the cheers of the crowd.

A dream I had envisioned more than seven years earlier had finally come true. Here I was, one of the contenders, representing the most powerful country in the world. We stood in the infield of the large stadium waiting for the remaining nations to join us. Country after country marched in until all were present.

Then a young Japanese runner, who had been born the same day the atomic bomb had been dropped on Hiroshima, came into the stadium. A great cheer filled the air as he made his way around the track and then climbed the stairs to where the huge torch awaited the flame. He stood there, the flame held high, as if awaiting the gods of Olympus to give him his instructions. Then he turned and faced the huge torch. The flame that had been kindled in Greece months before brought to life the Olympic flame of Tokyo.

The pageantry continued as a designated athlete took the solemn oath for all of us. The games were then declared open. Balloons and doves filled the sky and I was caught up in the moment. Somewhere in that multitude of athletes were my competitors, each with their own thoughts, each wanting the gold medal more than anything they had ever wanted in their lives. Also, amidst the crowd were Sharon and my mother and father, who had traveled half way around the world from a small town in Ohio to watch their son compete. I was truly overwhelmed.

The tension started to build as I realized this was to be my grand finale. All the sacrifice and dedication I had accepted, all those closest to me had endured. As I listened to the sights and sounds I knew that this was to be the greatest moment in my athletic life.

It had taken me many years to prepare and the time was now ... and the time was right. I realized I would never have another chance for these games would be the only time I could compete without a disadvantage. The air was clean and clear after the rains and I wasn't having any trouble breathing. It was going to be perfect. I was one of the best athletes in the world and was favored to win the gold. I felt great! Six more days before I'd run my trial race and I knew I must be very careful now. No more close calls. No injuries. I just needed to be sensible.

An hour and a half later we marched out of the stadium and boarded buses to return to the Olympic Village. It was time for the afternoon training session and it would be one of the last hard workouts I'd do before October 16th.

The track and field events were to start October 14th when Mills, Lindgren, and Larrieu were slated to compete in the 10,000 meters. The day soon arrived and it was every bit as beautiful as it was for the opening ceremonies. I watched the race from the television room in the barracks, along with more than 20 other athletes from the U. S. team. We were all wondering how the U. S. would fare.

"Bob, how do you think Lindgren will do?" The question came from Jay Silvester, a discus competitor.

"He won't be able to run as well as he could," I said. "He twisted his ankle a few days ago and it's still bothering him. The man to watch is Mills."

"Mills?" Silvester looked at me as if I were crazy.

"How can Mills do well? He hasn't run any world class times, has he?"

"No," I replied, "but he's a good runner and you have to remember that he hasn't a thing to lose. He has no tension on him and he can throw caution to the wind."

"Did you ever race him?" he asked.

"Quite a few times during the past year but I never gave him much thought."

Mills had made a statement before he left the States that the 10,000 was not his race. He was pointing toward the marathon, where he thought he had a better chance to place high.

I thought Clarke could win the 10,000 easily if he ran to punish the others. However, coming into the last four laps Clarke hadn't done his job, and now he was in trouble. Mills was still there and his adrenaline must have really been flowing. Emotion can work wonders and Clarke had allowed the scenario to take place.

During the next three laps when Clarke should have been going all out to drop his opposition he kept the pace even and allowed his competitors to stay with him.

After the gun sounded for the last lap, shouts filled the room. Mills was still in contention. When he came across the finish line with his hands held high, and then covered his face in disbelief, everyone in the room had trouble believing what they had just seen. The United States had won the first of many track and field medals and Billy was the first American to win the 10,000 in the modern Olympic Games.

The pressure was even greater now as newsmen asked me about the United States triumph. To win a distance race, even though it was an upset, made the odds even greater that we'd win another.

Bob Richards was one of those reporters. He asked me to do a radio interview that he'd tape.

"Let's just sit here, Bob," he said, as we made our way to a bench outside the dormitory. "I want to talk about Mills' victory and what that will mean to you." He turned on the recorder, then turned to me and asked,

"Bob, were you surprised at Mills' victory?"

"Truthfully, yes," I answered, "although I knew he'd run a good race. But I really had picked Clarke to win."

"What does this do to your chances?" Bob continued. "You have the fastest time in the world but an American has never won the 5,000."

"I don't think this hurts my chances at all," I replied. "I feel very confident I can win and Mills' victory doesn't change that at all."

"Bob, you're the only American ever to be the favorite in a race over 1500 meters. What pressure do you feel because of that?"

"Well, pressure has always helped me to run better. Being the favorite keeps me honest with myself. By that I mean I can't let down even if I feel very tired in the race."

Soon the interview was over and in a way it had helped. It forced me to put everything in perspective. Even though the odds were against the U. S. winning two gold medals in the distances, I knew my thoughts had to be positive and I would continue reinforcing my confidence.

I thought about all the telegrams I had received over the past week wishing me the best. One of these had more than a thousand signatures of Miami University students and professors. Many people had helped me along the way and they would all be watching. In the meantime, from the television on the first floor, I'd enjoy watching my teammates compete.

The next day George was to run in the steeplechase trials and on this clear, beautiful day, George ran the fastest race of his life, in 8:34.2. In doing so he finished third and qualified for the final on October 17th. He was also the only American to make the final.

On October 16th the sun was shining and I thought the Japanese had planned their monsoon season well. It was my day to run in the trials to determine who would advance to the final on the October

18th. As usual, I awoke at 6 a.m. I went to the track in the Village for an easy workout.

After some easy jogging and a few sprints over 100 meters, I walked back to my room. My race was at 3 p.m. After eating a late breakfast I went to the bulletin board to check the entrants in my heat.

There were four races for the 5000 with 12 athletes in each heat. They had placed each athlete in the heats according to the best time he had posted during the year. Since I had the fastest time in the world of 13:38, I was seeded first. There was some switching, though, to assure that no two athletes from the same country were in the same heat.

In my heat was Mohamed Gamoudi, who had placed second in the 10,000 behind Mills. Also Murray Halberg, the defending Olympic champion, and the young German Harold Norpoth, who had a best time of 13:48.4. They were the class of the field; the people I would closely watch since only three of us would qualify for the final. I wasn't especially nervous for the race.

Arrived at the stadium, I realized I didn't know where the U. S. had its training room. I walked around until I met a teammate who told me where it was. After leaving my spikes in the room, I walked across a bridge that connected the main stadium with the warm-up track, the same one I'd been using for practice.

There was an hour to go before the third heat -- my race. I saw many of my competitors already jogging. Jazy was there, but our confrontation would have to wait because he was running in the first heat. Bruce Kidd also was there but his unshaven face gave the impression he was anything but a contender. In talking with him I found my longtime rival had serious trouble with his Achilles tendons and had done little training in the last few weeks. He didn't expect to do well and was very disheartened.

I continued my easy warm-up for about 20 minutes. I was becoming nervous and decided to go to the main stadium. When I arrived I still had 20 minutes before the race and had 10 minutes before I was to report to the room they had set aside for checking in. Just outside the check-in room was a large dirt area I decided to use for my remaining warm-up.

Ten minutes went by in a hurry, and entering the small check-in room I could see the television on the wall with the race prior to mine being run. Bill Dellinger had been drawn to run in this trial and I watched to see how he would do. Bill had no trouble in finishing second to Mike Wiggs of Great Britain and I realized Wiggs was another contender.

Wiggs had run so easily he didn't appear tired at all after finishing. In third place was Thor Helland of Norway, who looked spent. Helland appeared as if he were running all out. Wiggs ran 13:51. Bill had run 13:52.2, and Helland 13:52.4, just four-tenths of a second in front of Lech Boguszewicz of Poland. The times were close but it was obvious that Wiggs and Dellinger were not really pushed and could have run faster.

Just then an official gestured for us to follow him. In single file the 11 other men and I made our way through the tunnel some 300 yards to the opening in the stadium where the ramp led to the start of the 5,000-meter trial.

As we reached the area we sat on benches to put on our spikes. I sat down next to Murray Halberg of New Zealand, the defending Olympic champion. I turned to him and said,

"Sure is a nice day for a race, Murray."

He didn't speak but stared at me, his face losing its color. I just wanted to stay relaxed but since he wouldn't talk to me my thoughts returned to race strategy.

My race plan was simple: I wanted to run as slowly as possible, therefore I wouldn't push the pace. I was going to run in last place most of the race and move up to the leaders with a couple of laps to go. I knew I had to be careful and keep a wary eye on the leaders.

We were called to the track, then to the starting line. The starter waited until we were placed in our proper positions, moved to his position, raised the starting gun, shouted in Japanese, and fired.

Everyone started at a leisurely pace and I fell into last position. Lap after lap the pace remained the same and at times I was five yards back of the nearest runner. I kept an eye on the lead runners, however, and with three laps to go I moved past the pack into contact with them. As soon as I was in good position my side started cramping and I wondered if this would be the beginning of the end. It was only a dull ache, however, as we came into the final lap.

Gamoudi was in the lead, Norpoth in second, and Halberg third.

I was running easily in fourth. The positions remained the same down the back stretch where there were six of us in contention. I knew there would be a sprint to the finish and I prepared myself by moving into third.

On the final turn Halberg came up on my outside shoulder and Norpoth moved out also. I was boxed. I'd have to run here until I hit the tape because Halberg wouldn't give. In a split second I made a decision to drop back, allow Halberg to go by, and then move to the outside.

I slowed and Halberg slipped by. Gamoudi was sprinting now and I knew the others would start at any moment. The way was clear behind Halberg and I had no trouble getting outside. I moved up to Halberg's shoulder and then moved in on Norpoth. I didn't care if I caught him or not and Halberg wasn't giving me any trouble.

I began to slow as we neared the tape and Norpoth was doing the same. I coasted and in the final steps passed Harold. I was in the finals. My side was in spasms, however, and I knew I'd have to do something about it between now and the final. I watched the fourth and last heat before returning to the village to see a doctor about my side.

I walked through the area where I had previously warmed up. The place was almost deserted because only a couple of races were left. On the track now was the 400-meter hurdles final and then the 100-meter final was to be contested. Just in front of me was Bob Hayes, who seemed to be searching for something.

"Bob, what are you doing?" I questioned. "Aren't you supposed to run the next race?"

"Bob, I can't find my shoes!" he said in a very worried tone.

"Can't find your shoes! Where did you leave them?"

"Here, right here!" he answered frantically. "Every day I leave them under this bench while I warm up." Then he stopped and turned to me.

"I know where they are! They're under my bed at the village! I forgot to bring them!" He looked at my spikes and I knew what he was thinking.

"I wear size 10 1/2, Bob," I said.

"Too big! What am I going to do?"

Just then Tom Farrell entered the area. Tom was in the 800 final, which followed the 100 meters. It was apparent what Bob was thinking, and he ran over to Tom and asked what size spikes he wore. I couldn't hear what they were saying, but within seconds Bob had Tom's shoes and was running for the check-in room.

As I waited for the bus outside the stadium I heard the final results of the 100 meters. Bob Hayes had set an Olympic record in winning the gold medal.

"Way to go, Bob," I said out loud.

That evening a trainer gave me ultrasound on the muscle spasm and a doctor gave me some muscle relaxers after he assured me they'd be out of my system within 24 hours. I had a good night's sleep and the next day, after jogging, was back in the training room to receive more treatment. The muscle didn't feel any better. I was worried. The trainers did everything they could think of to alleviate the spasm and by my evening jog, it felt better. I'd just have to wait and see how it went. These are the circumstances when I could use a Stubb Evans. I would talk to a top official about including such a person on future national teams.

When I returned from my jog, George had returned from the Olympic stadium where he had run the steeplechase final. I knew he had finished fifth in 8:38.2 and he was clearly disappointed. He had run four seconds faster in the trials and thought he could go a few seconds faster than that, but as in all distance races, and under these tremendous pressures and tactics, it's hard to run your personal best. He had run well and could be proud of his performance. Tomorrow it was my turn.

FIFTEEN

The Gold

Surprisingly, I slept well that night and awoke feeling refreshed on the day of the biggest race of my life. My spirits took a jolt, however, when I glanced out the window and saw rain.

It was just after 6 a.m. and I dressed to work out. Because I didn't want to run in the rain and take a chance of catching a cold I decided to jog in the bottom hallway where there were only a few people living. I had done this before when we first arrived in Japan. One morning I had a little trouble with an official. I was thinking about that incident as Russ Hodge and I jogged in the hallway.

It had been 6:30 a.m. and the team doctor had just said good morning as he left for breakfast with his cohorts. With the medical staff awake I thought we wouldn't bother anyone but in a few minutes a door opened at the far end of the hall and an irate official hollered angrily,

"What the hell do you think you're doing?"

Although taken aback, I spoke in a level voice, telling him we thought we'd loosen up indoors since it was raining so hard outside. He thought that was ridiculous and told us so in no uncertain terms.

"You are waking up my equestrian athletes," he continued in his raised voice. I thought he was the one making all the noise.

We apologized for making too much noise and offered to close the doors at his end of the corridor. He'd have none of that. He then stood in the entrance like a bulwark so the doors couldn't be closed. Russ and I were both irritated but we were not about to budge either. At that moment, as George Young was coming down the stairs having heard the entire conversation, I told the official we *were* going to run here so he might as well go back to his room. I moved away with Russ, who began laughing, irritating the official even more. With a few words I convinced George, who also had become angry over it all, not to pursue the matter but join us in our workout.

The hallway was 80 yards long and as we turned around to return to the official's end, he was still standing there. Before we reached him, however, he went back into his room, which was the smartest thing he could have done. Both George and Russ wanted to "let him have it," and I must admit my thoughts were likewise. We closed the doors to his end of the hallway and continued our jogging.

With the memory of that incident revived, I made my way to the first floor. I immediately closed the doors and used the other 60 yards to loosen up. It was an easy jog and didn't take long before I had enough. The pressure was starting to build and I tried to think of other things besides the race. I wondered if Sharon was on her way to Tokyo from Yokohama. My parents, who had flown in the day before the games began, were probably up as they were still early risers. It didn't work. I was still nervous and returned to my room.

George was waking up as I returned and after we joked about the weather, he went on to breakfast without me because I wanted to wait until 10 a.m. to eat, which would be my pre-race meal.

I relaxed on the bed, reading some of the magazines that had stories of my opponents. Many of these articles detailed their racing tactics but I was well aware that races of the past wouldn't be relevant to the one coming up. Anything could happen and surprise would be the key.

At 10 a.m. I went to the cafeteria to eat breakfast. All I had was cereal, toast, and juice. It wasn't much but it wouldn't be in my system by race time anyway.

Back in the barracks I watched some of the track and swimming preliminaries on television but after two hours the competition was making me so nervous I returned to my room. I lay on the bed thinking about every competitor in the race for the last time.

I was most worried about Jazy, since he was the silver medalist in the 1,500 in Rome, behind Herb Elliot of Australia. He had the speed I knew would be the necessary ingredient this afternoon. Then there was Dellinger, becoming better with every race.

I had predicted before we left Los Angeles that we'd win two medals in the 5,000. The others didn't worry me as much. I had beaten Bailey in setting the American record and Clarke had lost twice to me in indoor meets, having no finish kick. The rest were unknowns such as Kip Keino of Kenya, Harold Norpoth of West Germany and Mike Wiggs of England. They had looked good in the trials and could prove to be contenders. But Jazy and Dellinger were my main concern.

It was 1:45 p.m. and time to leave. I had two hours and fifteen minutes before the race. I hurriedly dressed not forgetting a raincoat and hat, and went down the stairs to check on Dellinger. He had already gone so I went out into the rain and walked the 300 meters to catch one of the Olympic buses at the front gate.

There were only four other athletes on board, and since there were no Americans I was deep in my own thoughts. Within 20 minutes we reached the national stadium and I pulled the collar up on my raincoat as I left the bus. The rain hadn't let up at all and it was so dark it seemed as though it were late in the evening, yet it was only 2:15 p.m.

I hurried toward the U. S. training room as the pressure continued to build. As I approached the room I saw Payton Jordan and Bob Giegangack, two of the American coaches.

"Bob, where have you been?" Payton asked. "We thought you'd overslept or something."

"I'm not late, am I?" I asked fearfully. The tone in his voice made me think I had looked at the time schedule wrong.

"No, no, you're fine. You still have over an hour."

"Boy, you had me scared, I thought something had gone wrong." I could feel the adrenaline pumping into my system. Damn, I thought, I'm going to need every last drop of adrenaline for the race. Then I smiled to relieve the tension and said, "I'd better get ready for my warm-up."

"Good luck, Bob, and run a hell of a race!" said Payton. Giegangack placed his hand on my shoulder, "This one's all yours."

Bob and Payton had always seemed interested in my progress throughout my career and I had always liked them both. It was support like this that was so heart warming.

I moved away toward the training room where I'd leave my spikes and rain-gear while I jogged. As I entered the room, Willie Davenport was at the far end dripping water. He must have just finished running his trial race. Willie had won the U. S. trials and was the favorite to win the gold medal in the 110-meter hurdles. I asked a trainer how Willie had done.

"I don't know, Bob, he just came in."

I made my way toward Willie. "How did things go, Willie?" I asked, expecting him to be upbeat because this would be an easy race for him.

His face was full of pain as he said, "I didn't make it."

This I hadn't expected and whatever had caused him to fail in the first trial, I now wanted to leave him alone for I knew he was emotionally hurting. But he continued speaking.

"I was fine over five hurdles and then I slipped a little in the mud and I got behind. Anyway, I hit the sixth hurdle and finished seventh." I could see tears coming into his eyes. He turned away a very disappointed young man.

Then the reality of it all hit me. After training so hard, for so long, something could easily go wrong. Twelve men would be racing for the 5,000-meter gold medal within the hour and no matter what would be said after the race the dream of each of them was to possess the coveted gold.

I remembered back to my early days of running in high school when I had been so terrified of competition. I had secretly prayed I'd become sick so I wouldn't have to take part. Now I was praying I'd make it through the race without mishap. The competition was still terrifying but in a different way. Now I *knew* what to expect. It would take endurance, speed, and most of all, the will to win, to decide the race.

It was now time to prepare for the race and since it was still raining, I decided to use the area under the stadium. Many other athletes were there when I arrived and the small 60 x 20-yard area was full of activity. I joined in the circle of athletes going around the perimeter and soon noticed I was followed by the two Soviets who had made the final. I stopped to let them pass and did a few stretching exercises before continuing. Within a minute I looked around and they were again on my shoulder. I knew it wasn't just a coincidence. If they were trying to unnerve me, it wasn't going to work. I was much too confident for that. I just complacently continued my warm-up. Soon they stopped playing their game.

Dellinger, Clarke, and Jazy were somewhere else in this vast complex, and I wondered how they were faring. With 20 minutes to go it was time to report for the final check-in. I returned to the training room and picked up my shoes then headed for the doorway about 150 meters away. Most of the athletes were already there, sitting on a bench in the order they would be placed on the starting line. I'd been assigned to the second lane and within minutes we were all there waiting.

The muted television in front of us showed the races preceding ours but no one was watching. No one in the room was talking, not even the Japanese officials. Everyone was deep in his own thoughts. You could feel the tension as we sat, side by side. I was leaning forward and glanced to my right. Jazy was looking my way and our eyes made a brief contact then he immediately turned his head. Still no sound. The tension was unreal.

I became tired of sitting so I stood and moved to the end of the bench where I could move around in the small space. Time was going by so slowly. I tried to remain calm.

Finally, an official motioned to us to follow him. The routine was the same as it had been in the trials only the actors were different. We walked beneath the stadium until we came to steps that led to the track. There were the familiar benches and we sat down to put on our spikes. Still, there wasn't a word from anyone.

I knew this was the only chance I had for immortality in the athletic world, for it hit me one last time that Tokyo was the only place I could have run in the Olympics. My allergies would never have remained dormant anywhere else with the pollen and air pollution that was prevalent in the big cities of the world.

There were only a few minutes remaining and I tried to move up to the track to loosen muscles lethargic from the 20 minutes of inactivity. But blocking my way were two officials who wouldn't allow me to pass. I had to be content with stretching while I waited.

Finally, they motioned us onto the track, and for the first time I felt the rain. It was a cold 56 degrees and it was so dark the field lights were on. Officials were busy pushing water off the track but as we came out they moved off and out of the way. There was only time for one run down the track before we were called to the starting line. The clay-crushed brick track felt slow. It wouldn't help us today.

We stood on the starting line through the introductions as the rain soaked us. The cold permeated our bodies and yet, as I waited on the Japanese starter to raise his pistol, it didn't matter. My thoughts weren't on the inclement weather any longer but on the task before me.

I watched the starter move to his position and raise his pistol. He spoke in Japanese. I tensed and waited. Within a second the gun fired and I took that first step. Norpoth, who was on my inside, was faster than me and he took the lead. Wiggs, coming from the outside, moved in beside Norpoth. Both the Soviets were running in lane two, side by side, next to Wiggs. I settled in back of Wiggs with Bailey on my right shoulder. I didn't want to be trapped on the inside but I couldn't get out, the way we were running. At this early stage it didn't matter.

We finished the first 188 yards and crossed the line which would be the finish 12 laps from now. We had started quickly enough but had slowed down. I felt my own body wasn't working well because of the cold and inactivity. My muscles would have to warm up again before I felt comfortable. How long that would take was uncertain but I was sure everyone felt the same. No one would be able to up the tempo, at least not for another lap or two. The track was dead; the rain had thoroughly soaked the clay-brick mixture and I knew we'd have to work extremely hard for everything.

At 300 meters Helland took the lead but stayed in the outside of the first lane as if he was hoping someone would pass him on the inside. But Norpoth, who could have come up, was content to stay half a step back on the curb. Dutov was third with Wiggs fourth. Jazy was running easily in fifth with Bailey following close to Jazy. I was running, without strain, in back of Bailey and could sense runners behind me.

Around the turn and down the straight toward the finish line the positions remained the same. Past the finish line, 11 laps to go. In the middle of the turn, I glanced to my right as Ron Clarke moved strongly past me. Following him was Dellinger and I found myself in ninth.

Clarke took the lead and Jazy moved out and up on his outside shoulder. Dellinger moved in front of Wiggs as he tried to stay close to the surging Clarke. He was still in the second lane and the pace had quickened.

Then, suddenly, Wiggs fell in front of me! I jumped to the right and barely missed his leg as I landed. Wiggs' spike must have caught Dellinger's shoe because Bill staggered slightly and then glanced over his shoulder. It happened in a split second and there hadn't been time to think. You just react to the situation. The runners in front of me had pulled away. I must close the gap, and quickly.

Clarke upped the tempo. I increased my effort and moved in on Bailey. Clarke looked strong and smooth. Jazy looked so easy. I felt good and knew I'd run a good race.

Keino was now running third with Dellinger fourth. Coming around the turn and into the finish line Bailey moved past Dellinger and I followed. As soon as I settled down Dutov moved past me into fifth. I stayed in sixth, in no hurry to jockey for a better position.

Ten laps to go. Around the turn and into the back straight approaching the three-quarter mark, Clarke led with Jazy on his outside shoulder. Bailey was back of Clarke and Keino in back of Jazy. Dutov was behind Bailey with Helland on his outside shoulder. We went around the turn and as we came into the straight, Helland swung wide and I quickly moved up, now just in back of Keino.

With nine laps to go Norpoth passed me and moved up to fourth next to Bailey. My mind breaks away to the noise of the crowd and I hear a chant of "Ja-zy Ja-zy Ja-zy!" The stadium seems filled with the Frenchman's people. As we go into the back straight I move wide past Dutov, Helland, and Keino to run alongside of Norpoth.

We go past the 1600 meter mark in that order and my body is finally moving easier. It's taken this long for my muscles to become warm. I can feel the tightness in my side but there isn't any real pain. If it stays like this I won't have a problem.

In the turn I move to the inside as Norpoth also moves in back of Bailey. Coming off the turn Bailey moves a little wide and Norpoth moves up beside Bailey on the inside. I'm in fifth. We have eight laps to go. Around the turn, we head down the back straight.

Clarke and Jazy are still running together although Jazy keeps half a step back. Norpoth is on the inside with Bailey on his outside shoulder. I'm now running in back almost between the two of them. I stole a glance backward and saw Helland and Keino side by side. We passed the starting line, then around the turn, and no one changed positions. We head toward the finish line and pass it with seven laps to go. I'm feeling no sign of fatigue, and, if anything, I feel better than when I started.

As we went around the turn I moved to the inside of the first lane and starting down the back straight, Dutov moved to my right shoulder. Now we're running in pairs, past the starting line and around the turn. Suddenly, coming off the turn, Clarke picked up the tempo considerably. Jazy stayed a step back as Norpoth and Bailey fell three meters behind. I must make a quick decision.

The way I feel it won't be any trouble staying with them, but I'm concerned about my side. The extra effort to increase my speed could bring about a spasm. I pick up my tempo slightly so they don't get too far ahead.

Clarke must be running on a 60-second pace now. My speed isn't fast enough for Dutov and his teammate, Biaduk, both pass me. As they go by I notice they're putting a great amount of effort into staying close.

Then Keino goes by and I wonder if I'm doing the smart thing. I can't allow them to get too big a lead. I must watch Clarke very carefully.

Helland now comes up on my outside shoulder. I'm in eighth place but I want to remain calm and keep the strain off my body. Around the turn with six laps to go. Clarke is about 15 meters in front of me but at this stage it doesn't bother me. The way my body feels I know I can quickly make up the deficit.

Clarke maintains the speed down the back straight and just as he passes the start he looks over his shoulder. I think he must feel demoralized as he sees how many runners are so close to him. He slows the tempo and Jazy, who had been a step and a half back, moves up to his shoulder. Norpoth and Bailey move in back of them. Dutov is fifth, Keino sixth; I pass Biaduk into seventh. Clarke is now just a few steps in front of me.

We go around the turn in that order. Coming off the turn Clarke slows even more. There's a domino effect as everyone in front of me slows very quickly and I have to chop my stride so as not to spike Bailey. Jazy's momentum carries him on by Clarke by half a stride. He glances at Clarke and slows. Obviously, he doesn't want the lead.

I move past Keino into sixth with Dutov to my inside. I glance over my left shoulder and see Keino on the inside with Biaduk on his outside. We're running in pairs again. We pass the finish line and have five laps to go. Around the turn Clarke retakes the lead but builds the tempo very little. The next lap is run evenly. We have four laps remaining as Clarke leads around the turn into the back straight. We're almost to the starting line again and Clarke shifts into high gear. He continues around the turn and then slows. Down the straight the tempo is relaxed. Just as Clarke passes the finish line with three laps to go, he slows again.

Jazy, with his momentum, moves to the front, but doesn't come to the inside. Around the turn he maintains the relaxed pace. Clarke continues to lag in the first lane. On the turn, Dellinger moves to my outside shoulder, but as we come off the turn and into the straight, I increase the tempo slightly and Bill falls back into eighth. We go past the starting point once again with Jazy half a step in front. Clarke is second on the inside, and Norpoth is back of Jazy. Dutov is fourth, with Bailey on his outside shoulder.

I move to the inside in sixth with Keino on my outside shoulder. We go around the turn. The tempo remains the same. Coming off the turn I feel trapped. I force Keino wide so I can run in the outside portion of the first lane. I will have an easier time getting free if someone ups the tempo.

We pass the finish line with two laps to go. Around the turn and we're into the back straight. I'm still running on the outside of the first lane so Dellinger moves to my inside. Keino is still on my outside shoulder. Something has to happen soon.

My thoughts are racing now. I can feel the adrenaline pumping into my system. It's time to move closer to the front. With each step I move Keino farther to the outside until I'm completely free. Then, with a little more effort, I increase my tempo and begin to move up. I'm amazed at how easily my body responds.

I pass Bailey and Dutov. Norpoth is third with Clarke in fourth. I move up on Clarke's outside shoulder and look at him as we go into the turn. At that moment Dellinger flies by me and takes the lead. For just a moment Jazy is caught off guard, but has no trouble increasing his tempo to stay with Bill.

We come off the turn and the faster tempo is holding, but it's far from what I'll be able to run. I've not switched over yet into my sprint style of running. I'm still in the easy stride that takes the least effort. I must be careful, very careful now. My thoughts are of my finish and when I'll start my kick. I'd like to wait until we have 300 meters to go. I have confidence I can maintain an all-out effort from that point. I feel so strong!

I'm still in the outside of the first lane and think there's no one who can block me. But then Keino moves up very quickly on my outside shoulder and Dutov moves up to Keino's shoulder. We're running four abreast and I'm trapped. Dutov continues his surge and closes on Jazy. At the bell, with one lap to go, Dutov is only a half-step back. Jazy looks at him and then, as if that was the signal to start the sprint, he begins to move.

My, God! No one can stay with him! Dutov is falling back. So are Norpoth and Dellinger.

The pace has picked up but with each step Jazy is putting more yards between the rest of us. In the middle of the turn positions begin to change and finally there's a gap I can get through. I come higher on my toes and drive into the wet track. I move to the outside and I'm free. Now I can run!

Out in front of me Jazy is still maintaining his lead while Norpoth has passed Dutov and has moved into second. I am in full sprint. I move past Dellinger and quickly close on Dutov. I pass Dutov and move into third. I'm in the middle of the back straight. The chase is on!

I can't run any faster and I'm not closing on Jazy. A thought goes through my mind that I have lost. But there can be no slackening now. As we go into the turn I move in on Norpoth and realize I have finally made up ground on Jazy. By the middle of the turn I'm by Norpoth and Jazy is only a few yards in front. It's evident he is tying up, his shoulders no longer relaxed. Coming out of the turn I'm only a step behind and I am confident.

Closer, I come to his shoulder as we fly down the final 100 meters. Several times he glances over his shoulder, his eyes wide. With 50 meters to go I pass him and pull away. The tape looms in front of me.

For the first time in the race my legs are becoming heavy but it doesn't matter now. All I can think about is what might be happening behind me. Is someone gaining? Drive harder, I think! LIFT... DRIVE... LIFT... DRIVE!

Suddenly the tape breaks across my chest. A grin spreads across my face. It's over! Thank God, it's over!

I turn to watch as Norpoth places second and Dellinger closes on Jazy. I can't tell who places third. Then I hear someone yell my name from the stands directly in front of me. I look up to see my wife Sharon, water and tears mixed together as they flow down her face. I reach up to give her a kiss.

As I turn around Helland and Bailey offer their congratulations. The area in front of me is filled with American fans and they're cheering wildly! I look up and wave.

Officials are trying to clear the track and one of them approaches me and speaks in English, but not well enough for me to understand. We're led off the track. Bill and I are ushered into a small room. We're told we must wait for the official announcement of who placed third.

"Did you beat him, Bill?" I asked anxiously.

"I don't know. It was close." he answered.

This waiting was agonizing. Our warm-up clothes and flats are brought to us.

"It'll feel good to get out of these wet clothes," I said.

"I was surprised it went so slow. How about you?"

"I was too," I replied, "but the weather sure was a factor. You know what, I wasn't even tired, with a lap to go!" A grin spread across my face.

Half an hour went by before an official walked into the room.

"Mr. Dellinger," he began, "You have been declared the winner of the bronze medal."

Bill looked dumbstruck. I looked at him and offered my hand. "Congratulations, Bill!" Nothing else had to be said.

"It's like a weight has been lifted off my shoulders," he said.

We hadn't put our warm-ups on as I didn't want to put them on over my wet running gear.

"Please follow me," the official said, as he gestured with his hand.

We gathered our belongings.

"Maybe we can find a place to change where he's taking us," I said.

We followed the official through some hallways to another room. Norpoth was already there. Several Japanese hostesses offered us juice. I saw a men's room on the other side and went in to change.

After returning, Bill went into the room and I'm asked to sit next to Norpoth.

"Bob, congratulations on your victory," Norpoth says to me.

I'm taken aback, because I didn't know he spoke English. "Thank you, Harold, and congratulations on winning the silver."

There's hot tea available and as my body could use something warm, I ask the hostess for a cup. Bill has returned and he and Harold join me.

One of our hostesses brings us programs and Harold asks Bill and me for autographs. We do likewise and I chuckle to myself thinking how this is truly a mutual admiration group.

As we sit there talking the emotional feeling is growing inside me as the realization of winning sinks in. Everything has come true. I had told the press before we left LA we would win two medals and we did.

Sports Illustrated and *Track and Field News* had picked me to win and I was the only American distance runner ever to be in that position. Horace Ashenfelter, in the 1952 steeplechase, and now Mills, were the only other Americans to win an Olympic event longer than 1500 meters. But they hadn't been pre-race favorites and their victories were considered upsets.

I had lived with that pressure for months and now that it was over, it was a tremendous relief. I'd done it! I'd won the gold medal!

We were told we'd have to wait until the finish of the 50-kilometer walk before our medals would be awarded. Minutes passed and a reporter from the *New York Times* came into the room and began asking questions about the race.

He was politely asked to leave since all interviews would be given in a separate room after the medal ceremony. He refused to go until several large Japanese men came forward, taking him by the arm and steadily moved him to the door while he vigorously protested.

Finally it was time. We followed a girl from the room to a door that led to the field. The rain had stopped and lights reflected off the water still on the track. We were in single file with an official in front and three girls in their beautiful kimonos back of us carrying the coveted medals on satin pillows. Dellinger followed the girls and I walked in the middle. We were led to the victory area, where we stood behind the victory stand. We were then told to step up on the stand.

The Americans in the stands, along with the rest of the crowd, gave us an ovation I will never forget. I knew somewhere in the crowd were my mother and father, feeling as proud as me. Without their support throughout the years, I wouldn't have been able to be here. I'm sure they never could have dreamed that their asthmatic son, with all his allergies, could have done such a magnificent feat. In spite of a health handicap, I had overcome the odds. Oh, I was proud, indeed!

My heart was full of joy as I thought about Sharon and this victory. She had backed me when times were rough and had encouraged me when I felt frustrated and disappointed.

George Rider; the man who had been my first real coach and had placed me on the right road, had to be proud. I would thank him when I returned home.

And finally, there was Igloi, especially Igloi. He taught me dedication and gave me the training that made the difference. Without him I wouldn't be standing on the Olympic podium waiting to have the gold medal hung upon my shoulders.

Over the loudspeaker came the announcement in Japanese, French and English.

"In third place, from the United States of America, with a time of thirteen minutes, forty-nine and eight-tenths seconds, William Dellinger." An official took the bronze medal from the pillow and placed it around Bill's neck.

"In second place, from Germany, with a time of thirteen minutes, forty-nine and six-tenths seconds, Harold Norpoth." The official took the silver medal and placed it around Harold's neck.

"In first place, from the United States of America, with a time of thirteen minutes, forty-eight and eight-tenths seconds, Robert Schul."

The Olympic official turned to the Japanese girl and lifted the gold medal from the cushion. I bent over so he could place the medal around my neck. He extended his hand to congratulate me as he had done with Bill and Harold. The Americans, located in front of me, were cheering loudly.

Then the official turned to face the far end of the stadium. All three of us turned with him and watched as the flags were drawn up their respective poles. Then the *Star Spangled Banner* began to play and the three of us stood at attention. Shivers went up and down my spine as I listened. I wished, in some mystical way, that all the people who had helped to make this moment possible could be standing here with me.

The realization of the moment hit me. It wasn't that I had won, for I had expected to win, but I was the first American to win the gold medal in the 5,000 meters in the history of the Olympic Games. I was the Olympic champion!

I had climbed the highest mountain
And stood alone at the top...
My dreams of days gone by
Would now be exchanged for memories.
I had run with the wind and,
For one brief and shining moment
The world was mine!

Afterword

As I look back over the past 35 years, the state of distance running in the United States is nothing like I had envisioned.

In 1964 after the distance runners of the United States had done so well, I thought we were into a new era.

Billy Mills had been an upset victor in the 10K, while George Young had run very well in the Steeplechase, finishing fifth. Bill Dellinger had placed third in the 5K We had arrived as a nation of distance runners, I thought, others would surely follow.

As the years went by we had some shining moments but nothing like 1964. Frank Shorter's victory in Munich in the marathon was a surprise and Joan Benoit's marathon victory in 1984 was an even bigger surprise when the top people in the world allowed her to break contact.

Now we have only one person, Bob Kennedy, able to run with the best people in the world. Why?

It could be said that the competition is so much tougher, and it is. I would be the first to agree that today's runners have to be better conditioned. But let us take a look at the differences.

First of all, runners run best when the competition is the best. It is easier to be competitive in a pack of runners. In 1964 that was difficult as the United States had only a few good people and if they weren't all in the race it became a contest of two or three people. When I set the American record of 13:38 in the 5000 meters everybody was in the race including the top Canadian, Bruce Kidd, and one of New Zealand's greats, Bill Baillie. The competition made the race and all of us ran closer to our potential because of it.

Secondly, I did not go to Europe in the summer where I could have found the better competition. That sort of thing was done sparingly and mostly when you were on a national team that would compete against other national teams. Starting in 1965, it became much more acceptable, possibly due to the fact that we had done so well in Tokyo.

Thirdly, it must be understood that we all had jobs to perform and if we were to train before a big meet, the athlete had to make the arrangements and everything was paid out of his own pocket. In

1964 only four weeks of training before Tokyo was paid by the Olympic Committee.

Today the athletes do nothing else but train. In the short periods of time that the routine was made available to me I can assure you I would have liked to have done it on a year-round basis.

Would it have made a difference? Of course it would. Not having to hurry from a morning workout to your job would have been a great physical and psychological help. Then coming from your job to an evening workout was even tougher.

Another consideration is the surface on which modern athletes compete. The cinder tracks in 1964 were always a problem. First, they were not as bouncy as the modern tracks which give you lift with every stride. Second, the holes made by spikes became a problem. As you stepped into them with almost every stride, they would tend to throw your body to one side. Therefore you were constantly fighting to keep the momentum forward. The energy this took away had to be considerable.

Three last considerations merit mention. The first is the equipment. The warm-up shoes we wore could not be used for training. They did not fit properly and they were too stiff. Therefore all workouts were run in spikes which created a different problem since they did not have support.

Also all the spikes were made alike and designed for sprinters. None had a heel and in the Games I wore a spike that was named "9.9". What does that tell you? I was the first runner to place a heel on his track spike to relieve the stretching of the achilles; within a few years heel wedges were regulation on all spikes for distance runners.

So the question has to be asked, "What would have been the time difference running on a modern track?" With all the things I have mentioned, with the same training, I believe that two seconds per lap is a good estimate. Therefore my 13:38 would be worth a 13:14 on today's tracks. That would place me in good company with most of today's American distance runners. With better training methods, better injury control and rehabilitation along with limited working, that should not be.

Second is the knowledge we have accumulated over the years how to train distance runners. I suppose the knowledge is really how hard we can train the human body. Throughout the past century runners have increased their training load in order to beat their competition. It is interesting that there was never a quantum leap forward.

For instance, when the mile was being run in 4:20 why didn't someone say to himself, "this is ridiculous" and double or triple his work load. There were a few who did more than others such as Nurmi and Kuts and a few others, but not to the extent of what could have been done. Were we afraid of injury? I know I was as I was always fighting an injury. But that had to do with my flat feet which I can blame on poor genetics. But my guess is that it is more in the realm of just being better than the competition and working to that level.

And that brings us to the modern distance runners. Is it that they are special people, genetically far superior to those of us who ran in the past? It is a valid question but maybe it has more to do with who they are and from where they come.

Who are these people who are running so fast? First they are not wealthy. They are driven by an inward desire to be better, to have a better life, to make money. They come from the working poor and they found a way to break loose from what their parents had to go through. They have tremendous incentive and obviously not everyone who tries makes it to the promised land, but if enough try some can surely make it.

What do they look like? They are small in stature, weigh 100 to 120 pounds and do not carry excess muscle mass. The calf muscle is almost non existent. My guess is that none of them could lift much weight. It means that distance running is not a strength exercise but a cardiovascular exercise. Nothing new, but we somehow have been convinced that we have to become stronger in order to compete with these weak, skinny machines.

So what do we do? How do Americans compete with these people. In my race in Tokyo, I was the biggest person in the race. I was six feet one and weighed 147 pounds. I can tell you there was not much fat on my body. Kip Keino was the only African in the final and he went on to win gold medals in 1968 and 1972. He was much lighter as were the other Europeans in the race.

There is no doubt that being larger is a detriment. It is like carrying added weight on your shoulders. Oxygen uptake is in direct relation to body weight. There surely is an optimum size that is best suited for distance running and my theoretical guess is that the Africans and Mexicans are very close to that optimum.

If we are ever going to be able to compete with this group of people we have to change our methods of sport in this country. Our system is set up to give the quickly maturing youngster all the benefits of sport. The small, immature youngster doesn't have a chance in our system, for they are the first to be "cut" from the team. These small-of-size youngsters could be the future of distance running if we can find a way of keeping them around until they mature enough to be able to compete. How do we do that?

This is where the Club system becomes very useful. But there are several problems. First we need well trained coaches. We have a system to train them now through the USATF but they would have to be monitored so that the youngsters could work to their maturity level and not be pushed too hard to "burn out." In other words we would want to be patient.

Then we would need competition for these people. That would be easier if it was cross country or road racing but if it was decided that track races were needed then it would be more difficult since clubs wouldn't be part of a school system.

Who would become part of the club system. All those young people who were "cut" from their organized teams in the school system. They don't have anywhere else to go and most drop out of sport.

How do we get it started? It would take leadership from the very top. Those people in the USATF who have control over the clubs.

Of course, these same clubs could be havens for others who are seeking better training methods like those who did make the teams in college but never reached the level of excellence they wanted. Maybe in some cases they never matured but now at the age of twenty-two they are ready for the hard advanced work. The clubs could invite these people to train with the backing of the USATF.

Now we have a different problem. These people would be coming from anywhere in the United States, seeking a way to become the best they can be. If we had a program where there were four or five distance running clubs in the United States, backed by corporations in the area, then help could be given. It would be nice if the various shoe companies would each have a training center. Most sponsor athletes but let others train them. They become a collection of talent throughout the United States and the world.

These older athletes would have to train four to five hours a day which means they would not be able to work a full time job. They would receive a stipend for being chosen to train. If the training centers were near a college they could work on advanced degrees. Otherwise they could work part time in local corporations.

I sincerely believe if I could train fifteen men and fifteen women under these conditions I could have a high percentage of them running with the best in the world within two years.

Epilogue

It is the winter of 1999-2000 and the book is finally printed. There have been many hurdles along the way, but as I said earlier, I am doing this for my daughter and her children.

In the past 35 years I have held a few jobs, starting with public relations, then being an athletic director for a club in Oakland, California. When the club went bankrupt I attempted a comeback for the 1968 Olympic Games. I had run through the 1965 season, but after being off two years, it became a good try only.

Then a two year stint as an assistant personnel director for a company in Oakland followed until I was asked to coach the country of Malaysia for a year. That was from April of 1971 to April of 1972. It was a very good experience but came back to a tough job market and finally decided to move back to Ohio where I opened a sporting goods store in the small city of Troy, Ohio, about 20 miles north of Dayton.

In 1973 I started the cross country program at Wright State University, just outside Dayton. We were Division II and in the fourth year we placed seventh in the nation. That was without any scholarships and a total budget of $3500.00 which included my salary.

After five years I became involved in an indoor tennis complex. It was in its fifth year when President Carter was elected and for those who remember, the interest rates went to 20%. People were scared and we lost half of our membership in just one month and eventually the facility was sold for a factory.

The sporting goods store continued until 1990 when the area had an influx of giant sporting goods chains. The small merchant was forced out and I decided it was time to go into teaching, the profession in which I had been trained in college. Starting in 1991 I was in the classroom in the Dayton school system. Then on June 14, 1999 I decided I had had enough and retired. At the same time I accepted the job as cross country coach at Wright State University starting in the Fall of 1999. At the age of 62 in September of 1999, I assume this will be my last job.

As I mentioned I ran in 1965 but not without problems. My knee began to have shooting pains when I started to get back into shape after the Olympic Games. Doctors could not find the problem and I nursed it along until February of 1965. Finally it disappeared but I had lost much of my conditioning.

The year became frustrating although I won the national championship three mile, setting a new American record of 13:10. That race was run on a leg that had a torn muscle, injured three weeks before. I had some good and several bad races that summer in Europe and reinjured the leg muscle in the last 200 meters of a 5K race against the Russians in Kiev.

After returning home I found the knee to be much worse than before and decided to retire, with regret. I didn't train again for two years until I began to train runners in California. At times I would run with them and the circumstances were such that when 1968 rolled around I found myself as one of the top eight in the 5K in the United States. I tried to bring my body back to where it had been in 1964 but at times I pushed too hard and would become injured.

It was a terrible experience leading up to the final trials at South Lake Tahoe. The trial race was agonizing, as I had an asthma attack during the race and struggled to finish fifth. I have written about those years and will publish that book in the future. In many ways it may be more interesting than this one.

All through the years, starting with a few athletes in California, I have had a Club team. Thousands of athletes, of all ages, have trained with me and I must admit I have enjoyed the experience immensely. I have also given my services to a few high schools over the years. At last count there are ten coaches in the Dayton area who went through my training program by running on a high school team where I was a coach or at Wright State or on the club team. There are others who reside and coach outside the area.

My own competition has been sporadic. Because of my flat feet I come up with more injuries than I would like but I still compete a few times each year. I very seldom go over 45 miles per week in training and that would be in the summer when I have more time to train. When I was 49 I ran 10K in 33:55 and at the age of 60 ran 17:55 for 5K and at age 61 ran 39:55 for 10K. Those times were accomplished on about thirty miles a week.

For all of you who have finished this book, I hope you have learned a little more about an era in United States distance running that was very special. To Jim Beatty, Max Truex, Jim Grelle, Ron Larrieu and to all the other members of the Los Angeles Track Club who made that club the greatest American distance running club of its day and maybe ever, I say *Thank You*.

Mihaly Igloi and his Hungarian athlete, Laszlo Tabori, taught all of us much about ourselves. It was a special time for American distance running and a very special time for me. All of us brought American distance running to the world stage. We were the vanguard and laid the foundation for all who followed.

My Best Times

440 yards -- :50
880 yards -- 1:52
1500 meters -- 3:40.7
1 mile -- 3:58.9
2000 meters -- 5:13
3000 meters -- 7:59.9
3000 meters steeplechase -- 8:47.6
2 mile -- 8:26.4
3 mile -- 13:10.4
5000 meters -- 13:38